SPYPLANE

Motorbooks International
Publishers & Wholesalers Inc.
Osceola, Wisconsin 54020, USA

First published in the USA by Motorbooks International
Publishers and Wholesalers Inc, PO Box 2, 729 Prospect
Avenue, Osceola, WI 54020 USA

Produced by David Donald
Aerospace Publishing Ltd
179 Dalling Road
London, W6 0ES, England

© Aerospace Publishing Ltd 1987
Color profiles © Pilot Press Ltd

First published 1987

ISBN: 0-87938-258-9
LC: 87-11062

Printed and bound in Hong Kong by Mandarin Offset

Motorbooks International books are also available at discounts in
bulk quantity for industrial or sales-promotional use. For details
write to the Marketing Manager at the Publisher's address.

ACKNOWLEDGMENTS

The author would like to express his gratitude to the following for their support and
assistance during the production of this book: Lt. Col. Bruce M. Bailey, USAF
(retd.), Jon Lake, Anne Skorzewski, David Mondey and Pilot Press Ltd.
The publishers would like to thank the following individuals and organisations for
their kind help in supplying illustrations for this book.

page 6: US Air Force **page 7:** Robert F. Dorr **page 8:** Royal Air Force Museum,
Imperial War Museum **page 9:** US Air Force **page 10:** US Marine Corps, Bruce
Robertson **page 11:** Imperial War Museum (two) **page 12:** MacClancy Collection,
US Air Force (two) **page 13:** McClancy Collection **page 14:** US Air Force **page 15:**
via Bruce M. Bailey **page 16:** US Air Force (two) **page 17:** US Air Force **page 18:** via
Jon Lake (two), via Robert L. Lawson **page 19:** US Air Force, via Jon Lake **page 20:**
US Navy (two) **page 21:** via Jon Lake (two) **page 22:** US Air Force (two) **page 23:**
Bruce M. Bailey **page 24:** Bruce M. Bailey, via R.L. Ward, Bruce M. Bailey **page 25:**
Bruce M. Bailey, Boeing, US Air Force **page 26:** US Air Force (two) **page 27:** US Air
Force (two) **page 28:** Lockheed, US Air Force **page 29:** Lockheed **page 30:** VF-102/
US Navy **page 31:** Lockheed **page 32:** US Air Force (two) **page 33:** US Air Force
page 34: Lockheed, US Air Force (two) **page 35:** US Air Force, Bruce M. Bailey, US
Air Force **page 36:** Bruce M. Bailey (two), via Jon Lake **page 37:** via Jon Lake (four)
page 38: via Jon Lake, US Air Force **page 39:** RAF Wyton **page 40:** US Air Force
(two) **page 41:** US Air Force **page 42:** US Air Force, Lockheed (two) **page 43:**
Lockheed (two) **page 46:** Lockheed, Bruce M. Bailey, via David Donald **page 47:** US
Air Force, Bruce M. Bailey, US Air Force **page 48:** via Jon Lake, via Robert F. Dorr,
Peter R. Foster **page 49:** US Navy (two) **page 50:** Lockheed **page 51:** Lockheed **page
52:** ECPA **page 53:** Bruce M. Bailey, US Air Force **page 54:** Bruce M. Bailey (three)
page 55: Bruce M. Bailey (three) **page 56:** Bruce M. Bailey (four) **page 57:** US Air
Force **page 58:** US Navy (two), US Marine Corps, Jerry Edwards via René J.
Francillon **page 59:** US Navy, Lockheed **page 60:** via René J. Francillon, US Air
Force, US Army (two) **page 61:** US Air Force (two), 100th SRW via David Donald
page 62: 100th SRW via David Donald, Bruce M. Bailey, 100th SRW via David
Donald **page 63:** Bruce M. Bailey (two), US Air Force **page 64:** Bruce M. Bailey

(three) **page 65:** Bruce M. Bailey, Lockheed, Bruce M. Bailey (three) **page 66:** Bruce
M. Bailey (two) **page 67:** Ryan, 100th SRW via David Donald **page 68:** Lockheed,
Bruce M. Bailey (two) **page 69:** US Air Force **page 70:** via René J. Francillon **page 71:**
Royal Navy **page 72:** US Air Force **page 73:** US Navy **page 74:** US Navy, Associated
Press, VF-102/US Navy **page 75:** Department of Defense, US Navy, Ministry of
Defence **page 76:** Swedish air force, US Navy **page 78:** US Air Force (two) **page 79:**
Associated Press, Chris Pocock **page 80:** Bob A. Munro, Lockheed **page 81:** US
Navy **page 82:** Terry Senior (two) **page 83:** via René J. Francillon, Terry Senior **page
84:** Terry Senior, Swedish air force, via Jon Lake **page 85:** via Jon Lake, Terry Senior,
Robin A. Walker, Terry Senior **page 86:** Peter R. Foster, via Jon Lake, Peter R.
Foster, via Jon Lake **page 87:** via Jon Lake (two), Terry Senior **page 88:** Peter R.
Foster, Paul A. Jackson **page 89:** Cpl Matt Trim, Swedish air force **page 90:** US Air
Force, US Navy, Grumman **page 91:** US Air Force, Department of Defense, US Air
Force **page 92:** via Jon Lake (two) **page 93:** US Navy **page 94:** Lockheed **page 95:**
David Donald **page 96:** David Donald, via René J. Francillon, Terry Senior **page 98:**
David Donald, 17th Reonnaissance Wing, US Air Force **page 99:** US Air Force (two)
page 100: Lindsay Peacock, David Donald **page 101:** David Donald (two),
Lockheed, Jilly Foreman **page 102:** Jon Lake, Lockheed, David Donald **page 103:**
David Donald, Grumman **page 104:** Tass, Royal Norwegian Air Force, US Navy
page 105: US Air Force **page 106:** US Navy (two) **page 107:** US Navy, via V. Flintham
page 108: Peter R. Foster, Jon Lake **page 109:** Peter R. Foster, Swedish air force
page 110: via René J. Francillon, Austin J. Brown **page 111:** via Paul A. Jackson **page
112:** via John W. R. Taylor, Denys Hughes **page 114:** US Air Force **page 115:** David
Donald **page 116:** R. Shaw, Lockheed **page 117:** via Jon Lake, Lockheed **page 120:**
Lockheed **page 121:** US Air Force (two) **page 122:** US Air Force **page 123:** NASA

CONTENTS

Introduction

Keeping an eye on one's enemies is the oldest military use of the aircraft, and it has developed into a highly-skilled art. Strategic reconnaissance has evolved as a distinct task within the aerial community, carrying with it the added glamour of espionage and covert activities. Here we describe the initial evolution of strategic reconnaissance, prefaced by definitions of some of the important terms used in this history.

Left: Undisputed king of the air-breathing strategic reconnaissance platforms is Lockheed's SR-71A 'Blackbird', seen here falling away from its tanker before climbing back to its operational altitude in excess of 85,000 ft.

Below: One of the most capable tactical reconnaissance aircraft is the McDonnell Douglas RF-4 Phantom, in service with several air arms. Tactical aircraft such as these sometimes return with intelligence more usually provided by strategic types.

Ever since man first carried himself aloft in balloons, he regarded the air above him as a perfect medium from which to watch his enemies during wartime. The advent of powered flight gave him far greater flexibility for aerial reconnaissance and, indeed, the first military use of the aircraft was that of reconnaissance. As aerial warfare developed dramatically during the early years of World War I, spotting and observation over the trench-scarred battlefields became the major role for the aircraft until more offensive tasks became possible. The art of aerial surveillance progressed rapidly, hand in hand with developments in performance and capability of the platforms. During this bloody conflict, the role of aerial surveillance over the battlefield became firmly entrenched in the spectrum of aerial warfare.

These pioneers of the art were the first exponents of a mission known today as tactical reconnaissance, and its importance is such that every air force with an offensive capability now sports tactical reconnaissance aircraft in its inventory. Some of these aircraft have phenomenal capabilities bestowed by electronic and infra-red sensors, while others still rely on the tried and tested human eyeball and black-and-white photography. Much slower in starting and developing is the role known as strategic reconnaissance, about which this book is mainly concerned.

The line between tactical and strategic reconnaissance is extremely fine and, at times, ill-defined. To begin, one should look at some definition by which to distinguish between the two. Current military doctrine tells us that tactical reconnaissance supports the theatre and tactical field commander and aids him in conducting the battle against an

Spyplane

enemy under wartime conditions. On the other hand, strategic reconnaissance enables military staff to assess the warring capability of the target nation during peacetime, and to continue such a task during wartime. It is obvious that such a loose definition can cause confusion: for instance, a dedicated tactical reconnaissance platform such as the McDonnell RF-4 Phantom could bring back vital intelligence about a foreign nation during peacetime, whereas the strategic reconnaissance platforms can bring back intelligence which is used by ground commanders fighting a war. Perhaps the best definition concerns the use to which the gathered intelligence is put. Tactical reconnaissance provides information for the ground commander, whereas strategic reconnaissance provides data to be used at high echelon or national level. The terms surveillance and reconnaissance also have slightly different meanings, the former indicating an effort carried out continuously over a long duration, whereas reconnaissance is used for an effort directed at a specified target over a short duration.

Several other terms will be used throughout this book, and these need defining. The data gathered by reconnaissance and surveillance is known as intelligence, and this falls into three branches. The first is Humint (human intelligence), which does not concern the aerial fraternity, as it is strictly the province of agents working inside the target nation, gaining intelligence by hearsay, visual sightings, documents and all the other devices glamorized in countless 'spy' movies. The second strand is imagery, which can take many forms. The most obvious is Photint (photographic intelligence), for which the aircraft has been ideally suited ever since the first camera could be carried over the enemy. Radar imagery can also provide visual data, as can the use of infra-red devices. Lastly, Sigint (signals intelligence) is the collection of non-imaging electromagnetic radiation, which too can take many forms. The two most obvious are Comint (communications intelligence) and Elint (electronic intelligence). The former is the collection of enemy communications transmissions, while the latter is the collection and analysis of *intentionally* radiated transmissions of a non-communicative variety. Radars are the chief targets for Elint, the receiver passively monitoring the characteris-

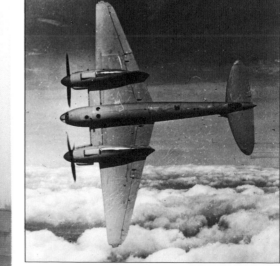

A German attempt to match the Mosquito resulted in the high-performance Messerschmitt Me410, which was widely used on reconnaissance tasks.

As with the Spitfire, the USAAF took to the Mosquito for its PR tasks. This PR.Mk XVI flew with the 653rd Bomb Squadron (Light) from Watton, a base later to see much clandestine activity in the days of the U-2 and Central Signals Establishment.

tics of enemy radar sets to assess their capabilities. Sigint also encompasses two other terms, Telint (telemetry intelligence) and Rint (radiation intelligence). Telint is the gathering of telemetry (guidance) data supplied to missiles and rockets. Rint is the collection and analysis of *unintentional* radiation, such as that from a dormant radar station, powerlines or even truck ignition systems. Rint can best be exemplified by the effect when a transistor radio occasionally picks up interference from a power drill or a motorcycle's ignition.

Strategic beginnings

While all reconnaissance aircraft use these various intelligence disciplines, the strategic reconnaissance fraternity have taken the collection of data by these means to the forefront of scientific and technological advances. The beginnings of strategic reconnaissance are as hard to define as the term itself, but laying a fair claim to the first such flights were the far-sighted clandestine missions over Germany made by Sidney Cotton (later Sir) in a civilian Lockheed 12A. Made immediately prior to the outbreak of hostilities in 1939, these flights provided first-class images of German ports and other installations and, although of limited use, these showed that the art of strategic reconnaissance could provide an excellent insight into the enemy's war plans. Cotton was instrumental in creating the Photographic Development Unit of the Royal Air Force during 1940, putting his pre-war experience to good use in setting up

Fast speed and rearward-facing armament made the Me410 Hornisse a handful in the reconnaissance role. Most of these served on the Italian front, plotting the slow advance of the Allied armies during the last months of war.

Spyplane

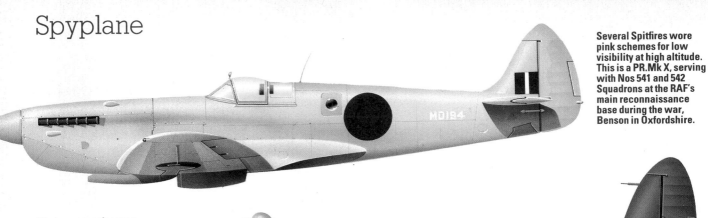

Several Spitfires wore pink schemes for low visibility at high altitude. This is a PR.Mk X, serving with Nos 541 and 542 Squadrons at the RAF's main reconnaissance base during the war, Benson in Oxfordshire.

Photo-reconnaissance Mosquitoes were used on long-range missions over Germany, where their performance rendered them uncatchable by fighters.

a group of Supermarine Spitfires for long-range reconnaissance over German-held territory. Fighting against service and political apathy, the group emerged as the Photographic Reconnaissance Unit and, as the war progressed, provided most of the imagery intelligence necessary to fight the war at national level. The Spitfires and de Havilland Mosquitoes operated by the unit became ever more capable, flying higher, faster and longer on their strategic missions over enemy territory. Learning quickly from the British advances, other combatant nations introduced aircraft to provide similar intelligence, and none took the art further than Germany itself.

High altitude operations

Flying unarmed on long overflights of enemy territory required that the platforms be faster and higher-flying than any fighter that the enemy could put up against it, requirements that would be pursued avidly after the war as the strategic effort stepped up. The ingenious German designers produced two types which could operate with virtual impunity over the United Kingdom and Soviet Union on reconnaissance missions. The first was the Junkers Ju 86P, a radical development of the Ju 86 bomber with a pressurized cabin, diesel engines and extended wings. Many missions were flown over Allied territory at altitudes approaching 40,000 ft (12 000 m), and these continued until 24 August 1942, when a specially stripped Spitfire Mk V clawed upwards from its base at Aboukir to destroy one of the Ju 86Ps based

Above: Successful for some while due to its phenomenal altitude performance, the Junkers Ju86P could carry out long-range photographic missions with impunity.

Above left: An idea which was none too popular was putting a photographer in a pod underneath a Lockheed P-38 Lightning. So configured, 'Information Please' shown here accompanies a Marines strike on Okinawa.

No 680 Sqn began life as No 2 Photographic Reconnaissance Unit in the Western desert. At the time of this picture it was in Italy, its Mosquitoes painted with a red and white striped tail to avoid confusion with the Messerschmitt Me410.

Above: Primary Allied reconnaissance type throughout the war remained the Spitfire, seen here in PR.Mk XI form. Note the battery of cameras in the rear fuselage.

Below: No 540 Sqn's Mosquito PR.Mk XIs were active from Scotland on missions against German shipping, and specialist surveillance flights over Peenemünde.

Spyplane

The Focke-Wulf Fw200 Condor introduced great range to the maritime patrol role, and was used to great effect against British shipping in conjunction with U-boats.

Left: Ground crew fuel a Kampfgeschwader 40 Condor at its base at Merignac in Western France. Much of the North Atlantic lay within reach of this mighty aircraft, including the all-important Western Approaches to the British Isles.

Below right: Lockheed's P-38 Lightning was a logical airframe to adapt to the photographic reconnaissance role, this F-5 conversion involving removing the nose guns and replacing with cameras.

Below: Captured by the Allies intact, this Arado Ar234B demonstrates the simple lines of the type. At its great operating altitude it was safe, allowing several important flights to be made over England at war's end.

on Crete for Mediterranean operations. Two further aircraft were downed and by 1943 the type had lost its advantage. In September 1944 the Luftwaffe flew its first reconnaissance missions using the Arado Ar 234 twin-jet bomber. These aircraft went on to fly many reconnaissance missions over Britain and Italy, their 39,000 ft (11890 m) altitude and 435 mph (700 km/h) speed rendering them uncatchable by Allied fighters. Such exploits did not go un-noticed by post-war designers.

Electronic warfare

High-altitude Spitfires, Mosquitoes, Lockheed P-38 Lightnings, together with their Messerschmitt Me 262 and Ar 234 rivals, all carried cameras as their only sensors. Elsewhere the battle of the radio waves was just beginning. Radar had advanced greatly during the war, carried aloft by bombers and fighters alike. The electronics specialists were soon at work to devise methods of turning enemy radars to their own advantage. German night fighters carried gear which homed in on RAF radar emissions, while specially-configured RAF bombers used chaff and electronic jamming to confuse enemy radars and give spurious returns. Such early electronic warfare laid a groundwork for the development of Sigint techniques and their direct application. Other developments during the war would have great impact on the growth of strategic reconnaissance after the conflict, not least of which was the use of long-range bombers as reconnaissance platforms.

The United States and Germany led the

Although underpowered compared with later jets, the Ar234 Blitz nevertheless could outrun and outclimb any piston-engined fighter, rendering it completely immune to interception on its clandestine flights.

Another German jet that could operate with little regard for Allied aircraft was the Messerschmitt Me262 Schwalbe. This Me262A-1a/U3 flew reconnaissance missions over northern Italy in 1945.

field in long-range bombers and patrol aircraft during the war, the latter mastering the art of maritime patrol with aircraft such as the Focke-Wulf Fw 200 Condor, which ranged far out over the Atlantic in search of convoys for attack by U-boats. The Junkers Ju 290 introduced even greater range, able to reach the eastern seaboard of the United States from its bases in France. In the Far East the vast distances between available airfields and reconnaissance targets meant that con-verted bombers had to carry out most of the flights. The advent of the Boeing B-29 Super-fortress and its F-13 reconnaissance derivative greatly increased the range and endurance capabilities of US reconnaissance outfits. More importantly, it was to be this type which formed the basis of the post-war reconnaissance effort, drawing on wartime experience in the Far East to evolve new tactics to be used against the Soviet Union, many of which are still in use today.

Long range patrollers, exemplified by this Fw200, and high altitude jets such as the Ar234 represent the two branches taken by post-war reconnaissance designs, one able to haul large loads over long distances, the other able to overfly hostile territory to bring back the intelligence.

Cold Warriors Aloft

Strategic reconnaissance grew up hand-in-hand with the Cold War, the importance and resources devoted to aerial espionage increasing as relations between East and West deteriorated rapidly from the end of World War II. The evolving discipline in the West was matched by advances in Communist defences, and the Cold War reached crescendo level by the time Gary Powers was shot down over the Soviet Union in 1960. This chapter describes the increasing level of activity leading up to the fateful shoot-down.

Left: No aircraft reflects the strategic reconnaissance role more than the Lockheed U-2. Extreme altitude performance was gained by the phenomenal wings, graphically displayed in this photograph of an Air Force U-2A.

Boeing's Superfortress provided the main long-range reconnaissance platform for some years during and after World War II, and gained much experience in Sigint disciplines. This is a Sigint-configured RB-29A, flying with the 91st SRS from Yokota in Japan.

Long before the conflict of World War II subsided, the Western Allies were coming to realise that they had no way of checking on the mighty military machine of the Soviet Union, which was gathering momentum as it swung through Eastern Europe. Although an ally, the Soviet Union was viewed with mistrust by both the US and UK, so that when the war officially ended in 1945 the chief concern, although unexpressed, was to find some way of monitoring the threat of Communist forces. Traditional Humint methods would be employed to provide much intelligence, but there were (and still are) large areas of the Soviet Union denied to travellers and locals alike. Aerial reconnaissance provided the obvious answer to this dilemma.

With its high-altitude Boeing B-29s the United States had the perfect vehicle for conducting reconnaissance flights over large areas of the Soviet Union, unhindered by any of the mass of fighters which the Soviets possessed. As relations between East and West deteriorated rapidly following the end of the war, these aircraft were regularly dispatched over Russian territory to keep tabs on military developments. The reconnaissance

F-13A, later redesignated RB-29A, was the prime variant for these flights, and this was later joined by the specialist B-29F, a lightened cold climate version equipped for long-range reconnaissance. Endurance was in the 30-hour class, giving the type great reach into the vast uncharted areas of Siberia from its Ladd Field, Alaska base. The United Kingdom also flew reconnaissance missions into the Soviet Union, using the new Avro Lincoln bomber, but little has been released about these flights. Shorter-range aircraft flew penetrations into East German airspace, and transports carried carefully hidden cameras along the air corridor to Berlin. Several aircraft that were attacked by Soviet fighters along the corridor were probably involved in espionage.

Sigint

Such flights, mainly using Photint methods, gave the West a greater understanding of the Soviet war machine, and throughout the late 1940s the effort was maintained. The fledgling Sigint community began operations with RB-29s in 1948, the first Soviet-targetted mission being flown from

Spyplane

Flying from Japanese bases, the USAF's fleet of RB-29As were active during the Korean war on many clandestine missions. This black example flew Elint missions targetted against North Korean and Chinese radars.

High altitude photographic and electronic reconnaissance was the domain of the giant Convair RB-36. This example is an RB-36E, converted to this form from the YB-36 second prototype.

Featuring uprated engines and a taller fin, the B-50 follow-on to the B-29 proved as useful in the Sigint role. Aerials protrude from many areas of this RB-50B.

to locate and negate this radar. Wartime radar-finding equipment was reinstalled in B-29s, and these had little difficulty in locating and classifying the ground radar, allowing punative steps to be taken. Throughout the rest of the Korean War RB-29s flew Sigint missions from Japanese bases. The Boeing RB-50G Sigint platform joined the effort in August 1951 flying from Yokota with the 91st SRS, providing the United States with a wealth of experience in this discipline, experience that would be invaluable as the Cold War became ever colder.

MiG threat

Photint missions were being flown sporadically over the Soviet Union between 1945 and 1950, but with the advent of the excellent MiG-15 these had to cease rapidly. The Berlin crisis had worsened East-West relations almost to breaking point, and the appearance of the MiG brought home to the West just how far the Soviet Union had advanced in military terms since the sadly-dejected horse-drawn armies that had vainly resisted Hitler's 1941 onslaught. The need for a huge reconnaissance effort was great, and the Western air forces answered with gusto. At first Boeing RB-29s answered the call, together with the upgraded RB-50 Superfortress. Both types began to carry ever

Ladd Field in July 1949. During the first months of the Korean War in 1950, Boeing RB-29s operated from Japanese bases alongside the bomber force, providing photographic intelligence. These operations were largely unhampered until November, when the Chinese entered the war, bringing their Mikoyan-Gurevich MiG-15s with them. The swept-wing jet fighter was one of the worst shocks that the West had encountered, being fast and high-flying, and out-manoeuvring contemporary Western aircraft. It also posed a great threat to bombers and reconnaissance aircraft when operating over the warzone. The MiGs were directed by ground-based radar, and it became imperative for the Allies

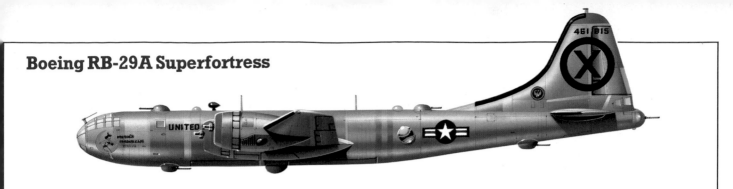

Boeing RB-29A Superfortress

The long range bombing exploits of the Boeing B-29 against Japan are legendary, and it was this long range capability that made the type perfect for reconnaissance operations. Initially designated F-13A, the reconnaissance Superfortress carried K-18 and K-22 cameras for Photint missions. Later, electronic equipment was carried, these being the first dedicated Sigint aircraft. As such, the Sigint RB-29As flew missions around the Soviet Union as early as 1948. A total of 117 F-13A/RB-29As were produced during and after the war. This is a Sigint aircraft, flying from Japan with the 91st SRS.

greater Sigint payloads, flying from British, Japanese and Alaskan bases around the peripheries of the Soviet Union. The US Air Force Strategic Air Command's newest bomber, the giant Convair RB-36, also joined in with both jet- and piston-powered versions being able to reach 50,000 ft (15240 m). Even greater altitude was attained by the RB-36-III, a specially-stripped 'featherweight' version which reached 55,000 ft (16770 m), safely above the ceiling of the MiG-15. A final B-36 version, the GRB-36, would achieve everlasting fame as mother ship to the FICON project, but more of that later.

Clandestine incursions

As the reconnaissance war stepped up the new jets were employed on clandestine missions. Many tactical reconnaissance types were employed on short-sharp incursions across the border, operating with scant re-

Above: These four North American RB-45C Tornadoes flew from Sculthorpe in RAF markings on secret reconnaissance flights over eastern Europe. Operated by the 91st SRW, they may have carried dual-nationality crews.

Below: Sliding panels in the belly of this RB-36D revealed large cameras, while elsewhere Sigint gear was carried. Several of the RB-36s were of the -III 'featherweight' version, stripped of armament to reach ever greater altitudes.

Spyplane

Above: Avro Lincolns were used for clandestine missions by several Royal Air Force squadrons, including this example seen in the Middle East. The belly radome housed special Sigint gear with which the Lincolns probed Soviet defences.

Above right: The English Electric Canberra carried out many reconnaissance flights from the 1950s onwards, at first carrying Photint sensors. This is a T.Mk 4 of No 540 Sqn, wearing a strange PR blue colour scheme.

gard for Communist airspace. In 1952 the arrival in service of the North American RB-45C Tornado added a new dimension to the West's intelligence gathering capability. The converted twin-jet bomber possessed much greater speed and manoeuvrability compared with the RB-50 and RB-36 and could reach an altitude of 45,000 ft (13715 m). These aircraft were used mainly in Europe and their success can be measured by the fact that, as far as is known, none were downed by Soviet defences during their operational career. At least four aircraft operated out of Sculthorpe in England wearing RAF roundels, although they were never on official charge. Under the auspices of the 91st SRW the four flew during 1952, possibly with dual-national flight crews, illustrating the close ties maintained by UK and US intelligence agencies.

The Navy joins in

The US Air Force was by no means the only Allied air arm involved in such activities during the first years of the decade. The US Navy was more than active in both Europe and the Far East, using mainly converted maritime patrol aircraft which, to allay suspicion, often operated in the markings of regular patrol squadrons. Types employed were the Consolidated PB4Y Privateer, (itself an

outgrowth of the World War II stalwart the B-24 Liberator), the Lockheed P2V Neptune and the Martin P4M Mercator. The United Kingdom maintained a large clandestine effort using Avro Lincolns and Boeing Washingtons. The last was a version of the B-29 delivered to the RAF to bridge the gap between the obsolete Lincoln bomber and the arrival in service of the English Electric Canberra. Other nations active in the strategic reconnaissance field were Sweden with Douglas C-47s, and France which at one point used civil airliners for reconnaissance purposes. Already the Baltic Sea and the Sea of Japan were becoming a veritable melting pot of clandestine activity, matched by ever more hostile defences.

Chinese interest

Although the Soviet Union had naturally been the focus of much of this attention, the 1949 Communist takeover of mainland China had made that country a target for Western snooping, particularly after the Chinese intervention in Korea. US aircraft were regularly patrolling in Chinese waters, while some overflights occurred. Many of these flights were launched from the Nationalist island of Taiwan, whose government of Chiang Kai-Shek was ever-willing to support these operations against their bitter enemy. The Communist Chinese were supplied direct from Moscow with MiG fighters and other equipment, and were no less reticent about attacking Western aircraft than their comrades to the North.

Indignation suffered by the Communist military, a vast improvement in their de-

Among the early types employed on covert eavesdropping missions by the US Navy was the Consolidated PB4Y Privateer. This PB4Y-2S served with VP-26, a notorious outfit which was to be the first to lose an aircraft in the espionage war. Note the plethora of 'bumps and bulges' which hide intelligence gathering antennae.

During the 1950s many tactical reconnaissance aircraft made border incursions to test Communist reactions. The RB-45C Tornado was a regular at this game, ably supported by fighter types such as the RAF's de Havilland Venom.

fences and the ever-increasing series of airspace violations by Western reconnaissance aircraft led to its inevitable outcome. This occurred on 8 April 1950 when a US Navy Privateer, serving with the notorious VP-26, was attacked and destroyed by MiG-15s while on a reconnaissance flight around the shores of Latvia. Ten men were killed, and in the course of the next five years a series of similar incidents were to take place. A US Navy P2V Neptune was the next to fall victim to MiGs, taking another 10 crewmen with it into the sea off Siberia. In 1952 it was the USAF's turn to suffer, with two RB-29s falling victim while on missions aimed at the Soviet Far East. Sweden lost a C-47 on a Sigint flight in the Baltic, the first non-US aircraft to be destroyed. One of the more publicized attacks occurred on 12 March 1953, when an RAF Lincoln was shot down by Soviet MiGs while flying through the Berlin corridor. Soviet reports insisted the aircraft was 75 miles (120 km) outside of the corridor and had paid no heed to warning shots. There is much to suggest that the Lincoln was on a deliberate spying flight. Incidents were reported sporadically afterwards, and for each one reported there must have been a dozen near misses that have never been disclosed.

Ferret flights

As can be gathered, the aircraft most at risk were obviously the Sigint types. Primarily Photint aircraft such as the RB-36 or RB-45C were rarely attacked, due to their greater performance capabilities which kept them out of range of the deadly MiGs. The Sigint types were usually converted bombers or patrol aircraft, not blessed with performance or manoeuvrability from the outset, let alone after they had been packed with bulky and extremely heavy intercept receivers and other Sigint equipment. Although perhaps no less hazardous than overflights, the missions of these aircraft often necessitated stirring up the defences by flying in provocative patterns, usually flying directly into hostile airspace to draw up the defences before about-turning to egress into the safety of international airspace, a practise which earned them their usual nickname of 'ferret'. How

many of the incidents concerning 'ferrets' involved them being shot at within Soviet airspace is unknown, for both US and Soviet reports of such incidents always differed. Most US reports included mention of a 'routine weather reconnaissance or patrol flight in international airspace', whereas the Russians reported a 'direct violation of our airspace . . . repeated warning shots which went unheeded . . . aircraft shot down so many miles within our territory'. The battle of words following a shooting incident could drag on for weeks, each side claiming the other in the wrong, yet still the 'ferrets' set out to deliberately goad the Soviets.

Overflight answer

Direct overflights had become extremely risky affairs with the gradual advances being made to fighters in the Soviet Union. Although still possible over the vast tracts of Siberia, the whole idea of using stripped down bombers for the job was obsolete. For the kind of Photint needed to monitor the nascent Soviet missile industry a new platform was required for the overflight mission. The US and UK found the answer in the English Electric Canberra. Continuing the tradition of British light bombers such as the de Havilland D.H.4 and Mosquito, the Canberra had a performance equal to the fighters of the day combined with ample fuselage

Although No.51 Sqn operated the B.Mk 6 as its main Canberra variant, other types were employed, such as this T.Mk 4. No.51 Sqn was mainly employed on Sigint duties: other early Canberras were believed to have flown overflight missions for photographic purposes.

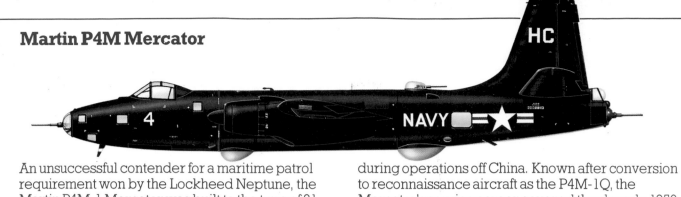

Martin P4M Mercator

An unsuccessful contender for a maritime patrol requirement won by the Lockheed Neptune, the Martin P4M-1 Mercator was built to the tune of 21 examples. None of them served in their intended role, going instead to equip Navy Signals intelligence units operating around the world. VQ-1 was the major user, and one of their aircraft was lost during operations off China. Known after conversion to reconnaissance aircraft as the P4M-1Q, the Mercator's service career covered the decade 1950-1960, and they were often employed on 'ferret' missions. What is not readily apparent is that they had two jet engines in the rear of the nacelles.

volume to carry large cameras. It is alleged that a specially prepared Canberra carried out an extremely hazardous overflight of the Soviet missile testing site at Kapustin Yar, launching from a German base and recovering in Iran. The flight was so hazardous that no further attempts were made, its failure leaving a gaping hole in the West's intelligence gathering armoury. By mid-1956 the United States had come up with two aircraft that could perform safely over the Soviet Union, the Martin RB-57D and the infamous Lockheed U-2.

Important changes had occurred within the Sigint community with the introduction of new types that were less vulnerable to attack. The Martin P4M Mercator had assumed the greater part of the US Navy's Sigint effort, allowing the ancient Privateer to retire gracefully. Although the P2V Neptunes of the regular patrol squadrons continued to perform clandestine missions, the Mercators of Fleet Air Reconnaissance Squadron One (VQ-1) handled the bulk of these 'ferret' flights. Formed in 1955, VQ-1 and its Atlantic Fleet sister, VQ-2, were to become the premier Sigint squadrons in the service, a role in which they are still most active today. The Mercators often flew with codes from regular Neptune patrol squadrons to hide their true identity: at a distance the two types bore a passing resemblance which might fool Soviet fighter pilots. In August 1956 a P4M with 16 crewmen on board

Far left: Intended as a maritime patroller, the Martin Mercator was only ever employed as an electronic intelligence gatherer. They saw more than their fair share of scrapes with Communist fighters, losing one aircraft in the process.

The Mercators were never less than sinister throughout their operational careers, flying either with no markings, or wearing those of regular Neptune patrol squadrons in an attempt to disguise their true purpose. No doubt the P4M-1Q's gun turrets were in action many times.

Originally supplied as bombers, four RAF Boeing Washingtons adopted a similar role to the RB-29As of the USAF, namely that of Signals intelligence gathering.

was shot down by Chinese fighters; another was attacked in 1959 by Soviet MiGs, although this managed to return safely. In 1958 the US Navy received the EA-3 reconnaissance version of the Douglas Skywarrior, and this allowed detachments of VQ-1 and VQ-2 to perform their missions from carrier decks. Lacking the range of the Mercators and other patrol types, the Skywarrior nevertheless allowed great flexibility, being able to operate from ships wherever it was required.

RAF stalwarts

The four Boeing Washingtons of No. 192 Sqn, RAF, continued their Sigint flights throughout the 1950s, gaining one of the most significant 'takes' of the decade by bringing back the first recording of Soviet airborne intercept radar, the rudimentary 'Scan Odd'. The Washingtons had augmented and then supplanted specially-configured Avro Lincolns in the Sigint gathering role, and served with distinction until 1958 when the first Canberra B.Mk 2s became available for the Sigint mission. More importantly, the revolutionary de Havilland Comet airliner was introduced to the RAF, which fitted out the capacious fuselage with listening gear and began operations alongside Canberras, renumbering No. 192 Sqn as No. 51 in August 1958. Other RAF units undertook clandestine missions during the 1950s,

among them the Signals Command Development Squadron at Watton, which flew a number of types on test and evaluation work, perhaps involving operational missions. More importantly, No. 543 Sqn, a wartime photo-reconnaissance outfit, was reformed at Gaydon with Vickers Valiant B(PR).Mk 1 aircraft in July of 1955 to begin strategic reconnaissance missions that would assess Soviet defences against penetration of the newly-born V-bomber force. Moving to Wyton later that year, the squadron flew its clandestine missions unabated throughout the late 1950s.

Still the prime exponent of the Sigint mission was the US Air Force, whose technicians and designers were introducing ever more capable equipment. During the mid- to

Strategic reconnaissance of Soviet approaches was the mission of the Vickers Valiant B(PR).Mk 1 fleet of No 543 Sqn, based at Gaydon. Fatigue problems eventually enforced their retirement.

For most of the 1950s the four Boeing Washingtons of No 192 Sqn, RAF, droned around the Baltic and other peripheral areas of the Soviet Union, their receivers tuned to hostile radars and communications. They served until 1958, long after the bomber Washingtons had returned to the United States.

Spyplane

This Lockheed RB-69A Neptune is depicted with a fairing for a side-looking airborne radar scabbed on to the rear fuselage. It is believed that this was the first operational application of the SLAR.

From the front, the USAF's RB-69 looked little different from the Navy P2V maritime patrollers. The hidden blisters on the fuselage revealed a considerably more covert role.

Described by the USAF as 'radio trainers' the RB-69s were frequently seen on West German and Japanese bases close to Communist territory, no place for a trainer of any kind. Overflights may have been undertaken, especially if the rumours concerning trapdoors for agent-dropping are to be believed.

late-1950s the USAF purchased seven Lockheed P2V Neptunes which were fitted out for the strategic reconnaissance role. These aircraft, designated RB-69A, were operated by the USAF as 'radio equipment trainers', but their real purpose was anything but training. Deploying from the United States, the RB-69s operated from German bases, notably Wiesbaden, and from Japan. Plying their trade around the peripheries of the Soviet Union, the RB-69s featured a plethora of reconnaissance equipment, including cameras and Sigint sensors. It has been suggested that these aircraft also incorporated a trap-door in the fuselage through which agents could be covertly paradropped into hostile territory. Later, during 1957, the RB-69s sprouted a long semi-cylindrical fairing scabbed on to the side of the rear fuselage, this being the

first side-looking airborne radar used operationally. The introduction of radar-generated imagery represented a giant step forward for the reconnaissance community. The Neptunes were treated very secretly, being kept away from the more public areas of the bases from which they flew. However, their 'radio trainer' tag did not convince many people: there could have been few more suspicious aircraft at the time than a Navy maritime patroller, painted almost black and sprouting a vast array of bulges, patches and aerials, and the whole contraption sitting on a West German airfield close to the East-West border!

Corridor courier

The attractions of the Berlin air corridors were still great, despite the number of attacks that had been carried out on Western aircraft using them, and a special USAF unit at Wiesbaden, the 7407th Operations Squadron, was equipped with two Boeing EC-97G Stratocruisers to perform Sigint during flights to and from Berlin-Tempelhof. This pair flew these missions from the late 1950s until 1976, when their place was taken by Lockheed C-130E-IIs. The entry into service of the classic Lockheed transport provided the USAF with another platform for its clandestine operations. Able to carry large payloads of electronic eavesdropping equipment as

Boeing RB-47H Stratojet

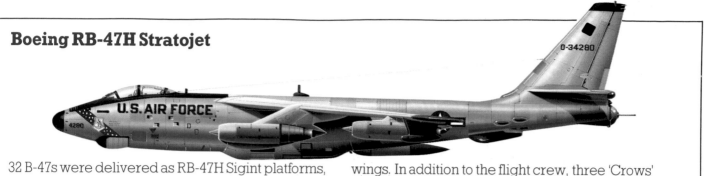

32 B-47s were delivered as RB-47H Sigint platforms, and proceeded to form the backbone of the United States' strategic reconnaissance effort until 1967. Powered by six jets, the RB-47H possessed high performance for such a large aircraft, although this was degraded by the weight of equipment carried and the drag of antennae added to the fuselage and wings. In addition to the flight crew, three 'Crows' were stationed in the extended bomb bay, complete with their reconnaissance equipment. All aircraft served with the 55th SRW at Offutt AFB in Nebraska, although they were to be seen in many part of the world on deployment.

well as cameras, several variants of the Hercules were used for reconnaissance purposes. The RC-130A was a photographic reconnaissance platform, but of more interest were the C-130A-II and C-130B-II, both of which were used for electronic surveillance. One of the former was involved in a bizarre shoot-down that probably resulted in the loss of 17 American servicemen. What is certain is that the aircraft was shot down by several MiGs near the Soviet Armenian town of Jerevan. At least six of the crew died in the crash, but the fate of the other 11 has remained a mystery to this day. The Soviet Union has never admitted shooting down the Hercules, while the United States intimated that the aircraft had been on a peripheral mission and that its navigation equipment had been interfered with electronically by the Soviets, so luring the aircraft over the border to make it a legitimate target. This charge had been made several times during the 1950s following the shooting-down of various Western aircraft.

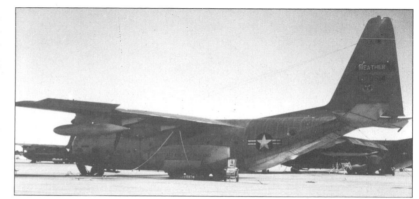

Secretive Stratojet

By far the most important new type introduced by the USAF was the Boeing RB-47 Stratojet. At peak strength SAC had 2,000 B-47 bombers in service, and the type's performance and range were beyond question. The 55th Strategic Reconnaissance Wing, the

Several versions of Lockheed Hercules have been used for covert reconnaissance missions, including this, an RC-130A. One of these was shot down over Armenia in 1958.
Boeing RB-47H of the 55th SRW displays its major Sigint antennae and receivers.

Spyplane

Above left: The crew preflight a Boeing RB-47H at Incirlik in Turkey. This base was regularly used by the 55th SRW's Stratojets, being close to the southern Soviet Union and its missile launch pads.

Above: Close-up of a RB-47H sitting on an English air base, showing the extended nose of the variant. British bases were used to launch missions to the Baltic and North Cape areas, where the 55th lost an aircraft in 1960.

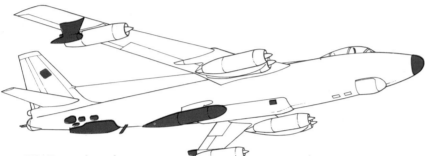

This diagram shows the reconnaissance installations of the RB-47H, including the giant pod slung from the starboard fuselage. Onboard equipment included the AN/ALD-4 Elint suite, together with attendant pulse analysers and recorders.

A proud crew stand in front of their RB-47H. The 'Crow' badges and name patches show this was taken in the United States, as these were never worn in the operational area. The crew consists of a pilot, co-pilot, navigator and three Electronic Warfare Officers (Ravens or 'Crows').

USAF's premier Sigint unit, had the job of introducing the RB-47H version of the aircraft to replace the elderly RB-29s and RB-50s operated for the electronic mission. The RB-47H was crammed with the latest equipment for electronic reconnaissance, including the ALD-4 Elint system. Other brand new systems were carried aloft as and when they became available. The 55th SRW RB-47Hs and their crews were perhaps the ultimate embodiment of the Cold War. The three electronics operators, known as Ravens or 'Crows', were housed in the slightly extended but nevertheless cramped bomb bay compartment. After fitting the recording and analysis equipment, there was virtually no room for the three men themselves, who had only rows of dials and each other to look at. Hours and hours were spent in these miser-

able conditions, yet the crews developed a love for these aircraft unmatched by many others. Despite the multitude of programmes ongoing during the late 1950s, it was the 55th SRW Stratojets that were the most vital and some of their discoveries were of major importance to the West, cataloguing the entire defences of the Soviet Union and keeping abreast of developments as they happened. The 32 RB-47Hs spent a great deal of their time in highly dangerous activities, either making 'ferret' intrusions or laying clouds of chaff to stir up some action. Crews got used to the sight of escorting Soviet fighters, always waiting for a slight navigational error to punish them with a hail of cannon fire.

Radical solutions

Apart from peripheral flights and the odd sortie over lightly defended areas, the Photint mission had been largely uneconomic since 1953, yet the need for it was growing greater almost every day. Soviet advances in nuclear weapons, missiles and long-range bombers needed rapid assessment and, as has been mentioned, by the mid-1950s a number of programmes were ready to fill the Photint gap. The US Air Force operated a large fleet of Photint-configured Boeing RB-47E aircraft, but these could not be expected to overfly the Soviet Union to bring back the required photographs. The most unusual programme to achieve this end was the Convair GRB-36. This utilized a B-36 motherplane which launched a small fighter that then carried out the reconnaissance run before returning to the B-36. Known as the FICON project, the fighter involved was the Republic RF-84K. Adapted to latch on to a belly-mounted trapeze carried by the GRB-36, the RF-84K had strongly anhedralled tailplanes and a hook structure on the nose. Together with a clamp on the trapeze structure, this held the fighter in place during the transit to and from the operational area. For launch the trapeze was extended, the fighter's engine started and when all was well it dropped away from the bomber. On

Above: Worldwide operations entail flying in all climates. RB-47Hs flew from hot and humid bases in Southeast Asia and the cold, dry atmosphere of Alaska and Greenland. This aircraft is seen in Alaska: the temperature is 50 below zero.

Right: Virtually identical to the RB-47H was the ERB-47H, which differed considerably in antenna detail, while carrying only two 'Crows' instead of three. Fitted with experimental gear, the ERB-47H flew special missions against Soviet targets. Three aircraft were converted to this standard.

completion of the assigned mission it rejoined the bomber, hooking back up to the trapeze which then drew the fighter into a recess in the GRB-36's bomb bay. The FICON programme involved some operational sorties during 1955-56 from bases in Washington state, in the North West United States, but nothing is known of the results or their destination. In any event, the FICON programme ground to a halt because of the launch and recovery problems, and the impending introduction into service of the RB-57D and U-2.

Ideas for a specialist high-altitude photo-

Below: An RB-36F was used during FICON trials, using a suitably-modified Republic F-84F as the fighter.

Spyplane

The cut-out and cradle under the fuselage reveal this aircraft as one of the GRB-36D aircraft used to launch FICON parasites operationally. Whether such missions ever involved overflights of the Soviet Union has never been revealed.

reconnaissance aircraft had been formulated in late 1952 by Major John Seaberg, and these resulted in the Bell, Fairchild and Martin companies being awarded low-key study contracts. Bell and Fairchild were to produce new designs, whereas Martin was tasked with developing their B-57 licence-built version of the English Electric Canberras an ultra-high altitude vehicle. Bell and Martin were given orders to proceed, the B-57 variant seen as a stop-gap until the Bell design could enter service. The basic Canberra already possessed good altitude and range performance, yet not quite enough for the overflight mission for which the new aircraft was intended. By replacing the Canberra's J65 engines with 10,000-lb (4536 kg) thrust J57-P-9s and extending the wing from 64 ft 0 in (19.51 m) span to 104 ft 0 in (31.70 m), Martin created an excellent high-altitude design. Twenty of these RB-57D aircraft were built, in three basic versions. The 13 RB-57Ds were single-seaters with large cameras aboard, and some sensors in the vacated second cockpit. A single aircraft from the line was the RB-57D-1, also a single-seater, which carried a high-resolution side-looking airborne radar for all-weather reconnaissance; the remaining six aircraft were RB-57D-2s for dedicated Sigint work, with the second cockpit occupied by a 'Crow'. Most of the aircraft were inflight-refuellable to extend their five-hour endurance.

The first batch of RB-57Ds went to the new-ly-formed 4080th SRW at Turner AFB in mid-1956 and flew their first overseas deployment late in the year to Yokota AB in Japan. Operated by the 4025th SRS, the big-wing Canberras also undertook missions from Alaskan bases. Project *Black Knight* was the name assigned to the RB-57D operation, and the aircraft flew many different missions, including air sampling flights at Eniwetok. Perhaps the most important of the operations was *Bordertown*, six aircraft flying from Rhein-Main in Germany on espionage missions along (and probably over) the Iron Curtain. Although never reaching the altitudes attained by the U-2, the RB-57D benefited greatly from having a much larger payload and available volume, particularly useful for Sigint work where the equipment was often bulky and heavy.

Taiwanese deployment

In 1958, as tension mounted between Communist and Nationalist China and the Bamboo Curtain closed ever tighter, at least three RB-57Ds were deployed to Taoyuan airfield on Taiwan. Crewed by Nationalist Chinese, and wearing Taiwanese markings, the aircraft flew over mainland China at great altitude, furnishing intelligence not only to the Nationalist government but also to the CIA. Of special interest to the latter was the emergent nuclear and ICBM technology being developed by the Communists. For two years the RB-57Ds provided excellent intelligence

This FICON composite is in its definitive form, with GRB-36D mother-ship and RF-84K Thunderflash parasite nestling into the belly of the bomber. Note the canted tailplane of the reconnaissance fighter, enabling it to fit under the GRB-36D.

on this and other major military developments taking place on the mainland, until a wing-crack problem forced their retirement. Throughout their service career the RB-57Ds proved admirable in their chosen field and, as far as is known, none were lost to hostile action. Their demise from front-line reconnaissance duties occurred in 1963, the high-stress on the overloaded wing spar bringing this about rather than any operational deficiency. After several aircraft broke wings on landing the aircraft were retired, some being reworked into EB-57Ds for ECM target work. Others were radically modified into an even more bizarre variant of the trusty Canberra, the RB-57F.

Johnson's 'Angel'

Sometime after Martin had received an order for its RB-57D and Bell for its new design (known as the X-16), an unsolicited proposal for a high-altitude reconnaissance platform landed on Major Seaberg's desk. The proposal was the Lockheed CL-282, mating an F-104 Starfighter fuselage with skid landing gear to outsize high aspect ratio wings. The inability to take the Air Force's recommended J57 engine led to a refusal by the Air Force to accept the Lockheed design, so the aircraft's designer, the legendary Clarence L. 'Kelly' Johnson, set off to find support elsewhere. Naturally the CIA were most interested in the CL-282, and Johnson agreed to enlarge the design to take the J57. After much debate involving defence, intelligence and government agencies, Johnson was given the go-ahead for his design in November 1954, to proceed in parallel with the X-16 and RB-57D. Production was swift, and by 1 August 1955 test pilot Tony LeVier was ready for the first scheduled flight ('Kelly's Angel', as the new aircraft had been dubbed, had made an unscheduled departure from the ground on 29 July during taxiing trials). The secret Groom Lake facility, high in the Nevada desert, had been chosen for the flight trials, free from any prying eyes.

Suspicious craft

The aircraft was designated U-2, the 'utility' prefix being attached to allay suspicion. If anything could arouse suspicion it was the U-2. A simple yet beautiful craft, it was engineered to the highest standard. Although the fuselage still owed a lot to the F-104, the empennage had been redesigned with low-set tailplanes and a tall, conventional fin and rudder. Whereas the wings on the F-104 were virtually non-existent, those of the U-2 were nothing short of amazing. Spanning some 80 ft 2 in (24.43 m), they were a cantilever structure built up around a three-spar torsion box, providing exceptional strength for low weight. In the main, however, the design centred around weight saving at the expense of structural strength. The U-2 could only take small amounts of load, from 2½ +g to 1½ −g, and was extremely tricky to fly at high altitude where stall speed and limiting Mach number converged alarmingly. No less difficult was the landing where the U-2's enormous wings, bicycle type landing gear (re-

Flying in company with a RB-57A, this RB-57D readily shows the increase in wing span characteristic of the type. Operated on a mix of Photint and Sigint missions, the RB-57D provided the USAF with a useful high-altitude platform before the U-2 became available.

placing the skids of the original design) and tall fin made it extremely prone to weathercocking in the lightest of crosswinds. The aircraft could not be thumped on to the deck as in most military fighters: it needed a carefully controlled power-off stall to settle it gently down to earth. Nevertheless, LeVier and his successors were excellent pilots, who took the handling problems in their stride, and flight tests proceeded rapidly.

By early 1956 the first hand-picked CIA pilots (employed as Lockheed test pilots for cover) were beginning their training. Come April and they were ready to begin operations. A year earlier President Eisenhower had proposed to Soviet Premier Kruschev an 'Open Skies' policy, whereby each nation's reconnaissance aircraft were allowed access to the other's airspace to report on military advances. Kruschev's reaction was negative and 'Open Skies' was never to be officially realised. Unofficially, however, with the air-freighted arrival of two Lockheed U-2s at RAF Lakenheath in England, the USAF could unilaterally follow the 'Open Skies' policy over the Soviet Union unhindered.

Operation Overflight

Operating under the cover designation 1st Weather Reconnaissance Squadron, Provisional (WRSP-1), the U-2s moved to Wiesbaden in Germany to be nearer the Soviet border, and to allay political difficulties then being experienced with the British government (it was the time of the Suez crisis). From this base the first U-2 overflight of the Soviet

No aircraft was to capture the imagination of the public more than the U-2, a designation which has become synonymous with 'spyplane' in most people's eyes. However, up until the Powers shootdown, only a few experienced commentators and enthusiasts were aware of the U-2's true mission.

66696

U.S.AIR FORCE

Spyplane

Lockheed U-2s furnished most of the important intelligence during the late 1950s, although the Air Force's aircraft played a lesser part in this, leaving the dangerous overflights to CIA aircraft. A wide variety of equipment could be uplifted, including most cameras and Sigint gear.

Union was launched on 4 July 1956. Flying over Moscow, Leningrad and the Baltic coastline, the U-2 brought back imagery which far exceeded the expectations of US intelligence experts. Any doubts that had been expressed as to the validity of the programme and of Johnson's 'Angel' were dispelled instantly. A second flight took place, which drew the first reaction from the Soviets in the form of a strongly-worded complaint. Such reactions became commonplace during the U-2's early career and were expressed in secret: the Soviet Union did not want the world to know its anti-aircraft defences were useless. The United States did not reply.

Missile watchers

Further U-2 operations began from Turkey with the creation of WRSP-2 at Incirlik (also known as Detachment 10-10), while the third unit, WRSP-3, took up residence at Atsugi, in Japan. Overflights from Wiesbaden (and later Giebelstadt) took place sporadically, until the German operation was moved in alongside WRSP-2 at Incirlik. The reason for this move was the Soviet missile test sites located at the southern end of the Ural mountains, which were to take up much of the US reconnaissance community's efforts for many years. Most of the U-2 missions were peripheral, being far safer and at times just as productive. From its 70,000 ft (21340 m) plus

perch, the U-2's cameras and sensors could look a long way into the Soviet Union. As the decade progressed, the introduction of the SA-2 'Guideline' surface-to-air missile forced the U-2 fraternity to adopt more carefully planned missions to avoid the missile sites.

The early overflights revealed much useful data for US defence planners. Among the most important was the fact that the Soviet Union had not produced anywhere near as many long-range bombers as had been previously thought, a fact which induced many sighs of relief in Washington. On the other hand, Soviet missile technology and developments were accelerating rapidly. U-2s were deployed to sample the upper air for particles from Soviet nuclear test explosions, a role performed excellently by WRSP-3 at Atsugi; WRSP-2 aircraft also deployed to Bodo in Norway for this task in 1958. Other operations early in the U-2's career involved monitoring the progress of the Suez crisis, while the first overflight over mainland China occurred in 1958. Nevertheless, the Soviet Union remained the primary target and many overflights took place; Detachment 10-10's aircraft usually flew from Lahore or Peshawar in Pakistan on these missions, coincident with a peripheral flight carrying Sigint sensors.

RAF and USAF interest

The first missions were all CIA flown and generated, but other agencies became involved in the U-2 programme. As good relations were restored with Britain, so U-2s began appearing at the RAF's Central Reconnaissance Establishment at Watton. During 1958 four RAF officers went to the United States to train on the U-2, although it remains a mystery as to whether they ever flew operational missions. What is clear is that by 1958 the British and Americans were again working hand-in-hand on aerial espionage activities, and the British were enjoying the benefit of much of the U-2-generated intelligence. The US Air Force had kept a healthy interest in the U-2 project since its inception, particularly as it had lost its Bell X-16 high-altitude platform. The 4080th SRW was operating the RB-57D, and experience in high-altitude op-

Whereas the CIA's operations were ultra-secret, those of the Air Force were less so, sending aircraft out on highly-publicised deployments on the HASP programme. These aircraft, designated WU-2A, collected nuclear debris from the upper air, catching the fall-out in a particulate sampler mounted in a cylinder on the port side of the nose.

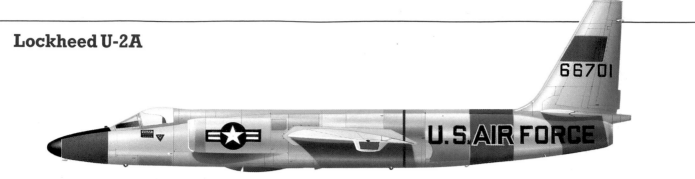

Lockheed U-2A

Designed by the legendary Clarence 'Kelly' Johnson, the Lockheed U-2A began overflight operations of the Soviet Union in 1956. Four years later the type had amassed a wealth of experience at this task, before Gary Powers was shot down over Sverdlovsk, so halting such flights. Overflights were handled by the CIA, although the US Air Force received aircraft for other reconnaissance missions in 1958. Power for the U-2A was provided by the Pratt & Whitney J57 turbojet although later versions featured the more powerful J75. 53 aircraft of the early U-2 series were built.

erations was deep. It had been the USAF that had supported the Agency U-2 operations at the three WRSP bases, and much Air Force money had been donated to the project. It was therefore natural that they should soon receive aircraft of their own.

Air sampling

June 1957 saw the first all-Air Force U-2s, delivered to the 4028th SRS, 4080th SRW at Laughlin AFB in Texas. These U-2As were shortly supplemented by WU-2As, which had dedicated air sampling equipment installed in the nose cone and an open ended cylinder on the fuselage side. With this equipment the WU-2As proceeded with a comprehensive global HASP (high-altitude sampling program) which, following a spate of above-ground nuclear explosions, provided excellent data on the spread and makeup of nuclear debris in the atmosphere. HASP continued into the 1960s, with publicized deployments to many parts of the world, including Eielson in Alaska, RAAF Laverton in Australia and Kadena AB, Okinawa. Apart from HASP, the Air Force U-2s also quietly picked up some of the Agency missions during the late 1950s, particularly over less sensitive areas such as Cuba, leaving the Agency aircraft to continue their dangerous work over the Soviet Union and China.

Francis Gary Powers

By April of 1960 rapid advances in Soviet ICBM technology demanded a series of overflights to determine their progress. One of Detachment 10-10's U-2s was launched from an air base near Peshawar in Pakistan to fly a reconnaissance mission over the missile sites, scheduled to end at the Norwegian base at Bodo. A further U-2 took off from Incirlik to fly a peripheral mission that, it was hoped, would distract attention from the overflying aircraft. The pilot of the latter was Francis Gary Powers, a Lockheed pilot flying for the Central Intelligence Agency. The date was 1 May 1960, International Labour Day, a Soviet holiday when defences would be at low readiness. Powers had little to bother him as he cruised northwards. During the photo run over the Sverdlovsk missile test site a violent explosion occurred beneath him, and the sky turned orange . . .

The CIA received the first U-2s, and flew all the overflights of the Soviet Union. Agency aircraft featured this sinister black paint scheme, and often flew with civil registrations. Some of these aircraft featured advanced ECM fits to help them deter Soviet missiles. This is a U-2C.

New Types, New Missions

The shooting down of Gary Powers' Lockheed U-2 sent shock waves through the aerial reconnaissance community, matched only by those reeling through political corridors. Aircraft designers, equipment manufacturers and tacticians alike were forced to seek new answers to the problem of how to get intelligence from the air. New types emerged which introduced phenomenal capabilities, while tactics changed to take into account the ever more capable defences.

Left: Tupolev's mighty 'Bear' set out over the world's oceans during the 1960s to snoop on Western ships, and to perform 'ferret' missions against air defence regions. This monster is a 'Bear-D', a multi-mission aircraft often encountered by Western fighters.

Despite the Powers event, the U-2 continued its useful career but would never overfly the Soviet Union again. This U-2A carries an ECM fit in addition to Sigint antennae. As the Photint mission became ever more dangerous, the peripheral electronic mission gained greater importance.

The shock wave of the SA-2 'Guideline' missiles exploding beneath Powers' aircraft was enough to overstress the frail structure, with empennage and wings separating from the fuselage. In desperation, Powers attempted to arm the self-destruct button associated with the ultra-secret sensors the U-2 was carrying. Whether or not he was successful was unascertained, but in any event the system did not work. Powers bailed out safely after failing to attain a safe ejection position. As he floated down by parachute to a Soviet welcome, little could he realise what shock waves the shoot-down would send through

both the political channels and the reconnaissance community.

It was to be four days after his capture that the news of Powers' escapade hit the world. What had been one of the most secretive military operations ever undertaken was now splashed across newspapers the world over. President Eisenhower stated that there had been no overflights of the Soviet Union, in response to which that nation produced Powers and his subsequent admission that he had been on an espionage mission. The cameras were displayed by the Soviet authorities, together with the pilot's personal

66701
U.S. AIR FORCE

Spyplane

effects. Tried in a Soviet court and convicted of espionage, Powers spent two years in jail before he was exchanged for the KGB agent Rudolf Abel on 10 February 1962.

Political leaders in the United States had a rough passage following the Powers affair, but the real shocks were felt in the intelligence community, which by 1960 was relying almost totally on the U-2 for major results. Following the shoot-down all U-2 operations quietly packed up and returned to the United States, never again to overfly the Soviet Union in such an overt fashion. Indeed, it was the end of overflights of such a direct nature: the only incursions since then have been peripheral or unintentional. Despite the furore and disappointment, the U-2's career as a spyplane was far from over. Air

Force HASP missions were still in full swing, together with a few of the CIA's less dangerous flights. The 'plausible denial' theory had been proved a wise one by the Powers event. Clearly the use of 'civilian' aircraft on overflights was far less dangerous diplomatically, as the US government could deny all knowledge of such acts, whereas to use an Air Force aircraft would be open aggression if the aircraft was downed. However, following the Powers event, the Agency was not willing to step up its operations in new areas where the U-2's talents were required. One such area was Cuba.

Reconnaissance breakthrough

Nevertheless, it was an Agency U-2 which brought back the vital first photographs of a major Soviet build-up on the island, and immediately flights were increased to monitor new developments. The Air Force wanted the task, and got it on 9 October 1962. Two pilots were selected from the 4080th SRW to convert to the U-2E, a version with extra ECM used by the CIA, and the first mission was launched on 14 October. This initial operation proved beyond doubt that Soviet missiles were based on Cuba. At the height of the crisis as many as seven missions were flown daily, and little could escape the cameras of the U-2s. Defences were strong on Cuba, and the U-2s ran the gauntlet of SA-2s and MiG fighters. The latter could only reach the U-2's altitude in a zoom climb, and they flamed out

Right: Even after the 1962 Cuban crisis died down, U-2s continued to monitor the islands, and have done to this day. This handsome aircraft is seen at Patrick AFB in Florida, from where many Cuban missions were launched. The date is 1963.

Far left: Their altitude performance led the U-2s to be used for many test purposes. This is a U-2D, complete with a second crew member seated in what was the Q-bay sensor hold in reconnaissance versions.

Below: This U-2 was specially-modified to drop canisters from high altitude for practise catching by Lockheed Hercules at low altitude. This simulated the release of data canisters by reconnaissance satellites.

Spyplane

Above: Reconnaissance aircraft gained their greatest success during the Cuban crisis, bringing back photographs such as these Ilyushin Il-28s returning to the Soviet Union.

Above right: The U-2R was used by the CIA over China. This silver example may be the prototype as it carries a civil registration (N803X) on the tail.

Exposed film from Photint flights needs careful and skilled interpretation on the ground for maximum intelligence use. These SAC staff pore over U-2 photographs taken during the Cuban crisis.

as they approached the high-flier, speeding past it as uncontrollable as a bullet before their kinetic energy ran out and they tumbled back to the denser air below. All the attentions of these dense defences led to an inevitable conclusion on 27 October when a U-2, piloted by Major Rudolph Anderson, was shot down by an SA-2. This led to flight plans being routed around the SAM sites to avoid them. Despite this, the 4080th SRW was to lose two more aircraft during the Cuban crisis, both to operational losses, one occurring when an aircraft disappeared over the Caribbean to unexplained causes.

Following the Powers affair the CIA U-2 operations had been seriously curtailed in most areas of the world, with the Air Force picking up many of the missions, as had hap-

pened over Cuba. One area which remained the 'Company's' domain was China. The demise of the RB-57D due to wing stresses had led the CIA to station two U-2s in Taiwan in 1960, and these operations continued through the early 1960s using Nationalist Chinese crews. Following the breakdown of Sino-Soviet relations in 1960 Chinese overflights were relatively safe, but in 1962 the first U-2 was lost over China. During the 1960s nearly a dozen aircraft were to be lost while monitoring Chinese advances in nuclear weapons: at one point Peking displayed four U-2 wrecks in the centre of the capital to show their success. The introduction of the U-2R model, again flying in Taiwanese markings, brought an increased capability over the mainland, and these continued their operations until 1974 when President Nixon's accords forced the cessation of all overflights. This was the final nail in the coffin of CIA U-2 operations, at which point all aircraft and missions were handed over to the US Air Force.

Sigint continuation

Several other moves were afoot during the early 1960s in the wake of the Powers inci-

dent. The focus on the peripheral mission became ever greater, and aircraft that were optimized for this became ever more important to the reconnaissance effort. In US circles prime exponent of this mission was the RB-47H. On 1 July 1960, exactly two months after the Powers shootdown, a 55th SRW RB-47H flying from Brize Norton was shot down by MiG-19s over the Barents Sea. This affair, hot on the heels of the U-2, proved as difficult for the United States, yet the peripheral mission continued unabated. RB-47Hs were aided and abetted by other versions of the

Above: Boeing ERB-47H aircraft continued their special missions, at least one narrowly escaping a shootdown.

Right: RB-47H 'Silverking' in flight. These were heavily involved during the Cuban crisis.

Below: An RB-47H caught at its Offutt base, with its C-135 replacement seen in the background.

Left: An EB-47E 'Tell Two' crew stand by their aircraft with most of their identifying patches removed. The conspicuous pods on either side of the nose housed telemetry data interception antennae. Most missions launched from Incirlik in Turkey.

Above: A little known reconnaissance variant of the Stratojet was the EB-47E(TT) 'Tell Two'/'Iron Work'. With two 'Crows' on board, these flew against Soviet missile launches, scrambling when news came through of an impending launch. This is the later version, with streamlined nose antennae.

impending Soviet missile launch to rush into action. These, the first dedicated Telint aircraft, were characterized by having two antennae on the sides of the nose to intercept telemetry data.

RAF involvement

Other dedicated Sigint aircraft active for the West during the early 1960s included the RAF's Canberras and Comets of No. 51 Sqn. Both types had been in use since 1958, and both were seen in a number of configurations. Certainly many different Canberras passed through No. 51 Sqn's hands, bearing a variety of designations including B.Mk 2(mod), B.Mk 6BS, B.Mk 6RC and B.Mk 6(mod). The Comet R.Mk 2s and their Canberra cohorts sometimes fetched up in Germany, and on Cyprus at the secret base at Akrotiri. Home base for No. 51 Sqn from 1961 was Wyton, which also played host to the Valiants of No. 543 Sqn and the photo-reconnaissance Canberras of No. 58 Sqn. Introduced into service in 1961, the PR.Mk 9 version of the Canberra was a high-altitude Photint platform, which although not possessing the performance necessary for overflights, was nevertheless a potential candidate for strategic reconnaissance purposes. Operating largely in the Mediterranean, the Canberra PR.Mk 9 was almost certainly used on missions of a clandestine nature, particularly in areas such as China (flying from Hong Kong) and over the Middle East. One other RAF operation may have included clandestine missions in its tasks, that being the equipment development squadron at Watton, which was first numbered No. 151 and then No. 97 Sqn. Primarily concerned with developing new equipment, the squadron operated Canberras, Lincolns,

B-47 bomber. One was the ERB-47H which traded one of the three Ravens for extra equipment, often of an experimental nature. Monitoring the Soviet missile tests in the south were EB-47E (TT) *Tell Two* aircraft (carrying two Ravens), which stood alert on the Turkish airfield at Incirlik, waiting for an

Above: The mast on the rear fuselage was a regular feature of No 51 Sqn Comets during most of their career. This aircraft is seen landing at Akrotiri on Cyprus.

Below: The Handley Page Hastings was used for a variety of equipment tests and Sigint missions. No 51 Sqn used this aircraft for the latter.

Above: No 97 Sqn continued the work of the Central Signals Establishment, flying a mix of types on ECM and Elint work. This Canberra B.Mk 6 (mod) featured a bizarre nose installation, and is believed to have flown operational Sigint missions.

No 51 Sqn Canberra B.Mk 6 (mod) basks in the Maltese sun at Luqa, the cockpit protected by a sunshade. The aircraft is in its second major configuration, with pointed nose cone and antennae on the tailcone. The weapons bay housed other electronic wizardry.

de Havilland Comet R.Mk 2

During 1958 the first Comets entered service with the RAF's No 192 Sqn at Wyton. No 192 renumbered as No 51 Sqn soon after, and the Comets served on the unit until 1974. Some seven airframes were used by this unit at one time or another, and they were highly active on clandestine missions around the periphery of the Soviet Union and its Allies. A favourite haunt was in southern Europe, operating from Mediterranean bases in addition to others in Turkey and Iran. Particular attention was paid to radar activity, and in this role the Comets replaced the Boeing Washingtons used previously.

Left: Seen with the later rounded nose cone, this B.Mk 6 (mod) Canberra awaits a mission at an airfield somewhere on the Persian Gulf.

Right: High-altitude photo-reconnaissance for the Royal Air Force was handled by various Canberra variants, led by the PR.Mk 9 with uprated engines and enlarged wings. The navigator sat in the nose, the black markings being a frangible panel through which he ejected.

Below: Since the early 1960s, NATO fighter pilots have become familiar with the awesome sight of the Tupolev Tu-95 'Bear' as they probe air defence regions. This 'Bear-B' was caught by a Convair F-102 along the eastern seaboard of the United States.

Vikings and Handley Page Hastings until 1967.

One notable absentee from the international strategic reconnaissance scene until 1960 was the Soviet Union itself, long the victim of overflights, 'ferret' missions and peripheral snooping. As the decade started the Soviets felt it time to send their long-range bomber trio out into the world to perform similar duties around Western navies and coastlines. Tupolev Tu-16 'Badgers', Tu-95 'Bears' and Myasishchev Mya-4 'Bisons' became regular sights around Western naval formations, all equipped for photographic reconnaissance and also to lap up electromagnetic radiation emitted by the Western ships. The Soviet aircraft began operations from Egyptian bases to monitor Western developments in the Mediterranean. Such activities rapidly became an accepted part of the overall reconnaissance scene, increasing in regularity until their operations equalled or even overtook those of the West.

Myasishchev Mya-4 'Bison'

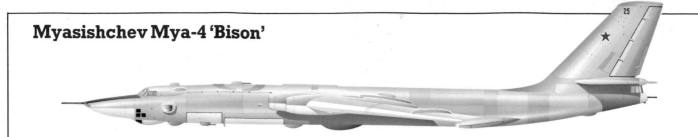

Least known of the Soviet bomber trio, the Mya-4 has nevertheless played an important part in reconnaissance activities. A major feat of engineering for its day, the 'Bison' features four powerful Mikulin turbojets buried in the wing roots and a bicycle-type undercarriage with wingtip outriggers. Many of the original bombers were converted to 'Bison-B' or 'Bison-C' reconnaissance standard, the latter having a large radar in a pointed nose. Both recon versions feature cameras and a wealth of Sigint equipment for cataloguing Western naval radars, while they also take part in 'ferret' activities.

Left: This head-on view serves to illustrate the outsize wings and TF33 turbofan engines of the Martin RB-57F. Combined with the extra turbojets under the wings, these features could take a large payload of sensors to extreme altitude.

Below: Featuring an enlarged sensor bay, this RB-57F is operating without the auxiliary J60 turbojets. Most of the RB-57Fs had a brief operational career before conversion to WB-57F weather reconnaissance platforms.

The successes of the U-2 had driven the Soviet Union to develop its own high-altitude reconnaissance platform, the Yakovlev Yak-25RD (or Yak-26) 'Mandrake', which married the fuselage of the Yak-25 twin-engined fighter with outsize wings. Although never matching the success or performance of the U-2, the 'Mandrake' was used from 1963 on espionage flights over China, India and Pakistan, but never over the heavily-defended areas of Europe. Even these countries soon had defences good enough to render the Yak aircraft useless for overflights and its appearance on the reconnaissance scene appears to have been brief.

Outsize wings

Other high-altitude projects in the United States led to further modification of the B-57 airframe to RB-57F standard. This aircraft was almost unrecognisable from its Canberra forebear, having a phenomenal 121 ft (36.88 m) wing, giant TF33 engines and two extra J60 jets carried in pods under the wing. To cope with the extra wing area and power the fin was increased dramatically in area. General Dynamics carried out the modifications and the first aircraft was delivered to the US Air Force in 1963. Able to carry an immense payload, including the revolutionary HIAC long-range oblique camera, the RB-57F could reach almost 80,000 ft (24400 m). RB-57Fs went into service with the 7407th SS in Germany and later began operations from Yokota in Japan. The former lost an aircraft in mysterious circumstances over the Black Sea on 14 December 1965, reportedly to an SA-2 missile in international airspace. Other RB-57F aircraft surfaced in Pakistan, where their altitude performance made them excellent platforms for assessing Indian military power during the 1965 war between the two nations. Two aircraft were used by Pakistan, one of which was seriously damaged by Indian SA-2s during the course of a reconnaissance mission, and there is much speculation that they were flying under the auspices of the CIA. The RB-57Fs ended their service days as WB-57F weather reconnaissance aircraft, a role which had been used

Yakovlev Yak-25RD 'Mandrake'

The Soviet counterpart of the Lockheed U-2 was a rebuild of the Yak-25 fighter with outsize wings to give it high altitude performance. Although never rivalling the Lockheed design on performance, the 'Mandrake' undertook several reconnaissance flights during the early 1960s, and was even intercepted by Western aircraft. Equipment included both Photint and Elint sensors. Few details are available; even the designation is speculative as some agencies quote Yak-26 as the correct one. The number of conversions is unknown, although it is thought to only number a handful.

earlier as a cover during their more active career.

Such programmes were small fry compared to that being undertaken at Lockheed's famous 'Skunk Works', which had produced the U-2. A family of aircraft would emerge from this secret establishment that would represent the height of aviation development: the 'Blackbirds'. For some time this unit and its prime mover, 'Kelly' Johnson, had been investigating liquid hydrogen powered aircraft as a means of obtaining phenomenal performance. Although work was progressing rapidly, by 1957 Johnson had come to doubt the feasibility of liquid hydrogen power, and the project was cancelled in favour of a more conventional aircraft. This new programme was funded by the CIA, and despite proposals from other manufacturers the CIA elected to proceed with Lockheed, with whom it had worked hand-in-hand over the eminently successful U-2 programme. Johnson had prepared a series of preliminary designs (A-1 to A-12) during the

The vast wing area of the RB-57F is readily apparent in this view, as is the crude enlarged fin which was fitted to cope with the extra power and wing. Sensors were carried in the fuselage bay, among them the giant HIAC camera, developed specifically for the RB-57F.

Spyplane

Left: Three A-12s were developed as YF-12A interceptors, with fire control radar in a large radome, and infra-red sensor balls in the forward chines. Despite a lengthy evaluation, the fighter version was relegated to NASA high speed trials flights.

Above: The single seat cockpit, short tailcone and slender nose profile identify this as an A-12, used operationally before the SR-71A took over the mission. Sensors were carried largely in the chine area.

Below: Two A-12s were converted to carry the Mach 4 Lockheed D-21 drone, with a central pylon and a second cockpit for the launch control officer. Note the black painted nose, chines and leading edges of the A-12.

late 1950s, and work was soon progressing rapidly on the A-12 design to the extent that it was complete by January 1962.

Transported by road to the Groom Lake facility in Nevada that had seen the major part of the U-2 flight test programme, the A-12 was assembled and readied for its first flight. This occurred unofficially on 24 April during a high-speed taxi run, with the official full first flight taking place two days later with Lou Schalk at the controls. The A-12 was an impressive machine by any account. Basically a delta, two huge engine nacelles were faired into the wing with streamlined chines, and these features were incorporated into the basic cylindrical fuselage structure. The fuselage chines blended into the leading edge of the wing, giving the A-12 the appear-

ance of a demented sea monster rather than an aeroplane. Two giant angular slab fins sat on top of the engine nacelles, canted inwards to complete the radical look of the secret aircraft. Initial flight tests showed no major aerodynamic problems, yet the proposed Pratt & Whitney J58 turbojets were not yet ready, so the A-12 flew for the first months powered by two J75 engines. Eventually the J58 was fitted, and a myriad of problems surfaced which dogged the A-12 programme for many months. Chief among these was the propulsive system, each engine requiring superfine control of the airflow by several rows of inlet and outlet doors, together with careful positioning of the giant inlet spike, which travelled forward and aft throughout the flight regime for optimum positioning of the huge shock wave which built up in front of the inlets at high speeds.

A-12 into service

Despite these problems the CIA quickly put the A-12 into use on reconnaissance missions, but virtually nothing is known of their activities. It is believed that they were operated over China and Vietnam and remained in service until 1967-68, by which time their missions were taken over by the SR-71. The basic A-12 was a single seater, and carried its sensors in the nose section, chine areas and a Q-bay behind the cockpit. Fifteen were built for the CIA, of which at least six were thought to be lost in accidents. One aircraft incorporated a second raised cockpit for training

purposes, and two aircraft were configured for the even more secret D-21 drone programme. The D-21 was a Mach 4 ramjet-powered drone which borrowed aerodynamic features from the A-12, a bat-shaped aircraft resembling a winged A-12 engine nacelle. It was carried on a special pylon mounted on the rear fuselage spine of the A-12 and launched at speed and altitude to begin its penetration of extremely hostile airspace, after which it ejected a canister containing the gathered intelligence before being expended. Control during launch was provided by a second crew member stationed in a cabin immediately behind the A-12's pilot. The A-12 period of the D-21's history seems to be an unhappy one, with one of the aircraft being lost during a drone launch when the D-21 flew back into the A-12. Subsequent testing was accomplished from the underwing pylons of Boeing B-52H bombers serving with the 4200th Test Wing at Beale AFB in California, and this combination probably saw limited operational service over China and Vietnam in the mid- to late-1960s. What degree of success was obtained by the D-21 remains hidden in the vaults of the CIA, and the programme terminated before reaching any large scale use.

Fighter derivative

Second in the 'Blackbird' line was the YF-12A, which was a fighter derivative of the A-12 with a long-range Hughes radar in the nose and associated forward-looking infra-red sensors. AIM-47 missiles were carried in fuselage bays and a second cockpit was added for the Weapons Systems Officer. Although considerably slower than the A-12, it was a YF-12A that was used to set world records for speed and altitude. Widely tested, the YF-12A programme amounted only to three aircraft, and these were relegated to general high altitude trials at Edwards AFB and then with NASA.

Despite its phenomenal performance the

Lockheed SR-71A 'Blackbird'

It is indicative of the importance of strategic reconnaissance that the world's fastest and highest-flying air-breathing aircraft was developed specifically to perform the task. Developed from the A-12, the SR-71A made its operational debut in 1966, and has been kept more than busy ever since. The structure is largely made from titanium alloys to withstand the heat generated at the Mach 3 operating speeds, while the fuselage expands several inches at full speed. A wide variety of sensors can be carried in the nose and chine areas, controlled either by automatic mission cassettes or from the Reconnaissance Systems Officer station.

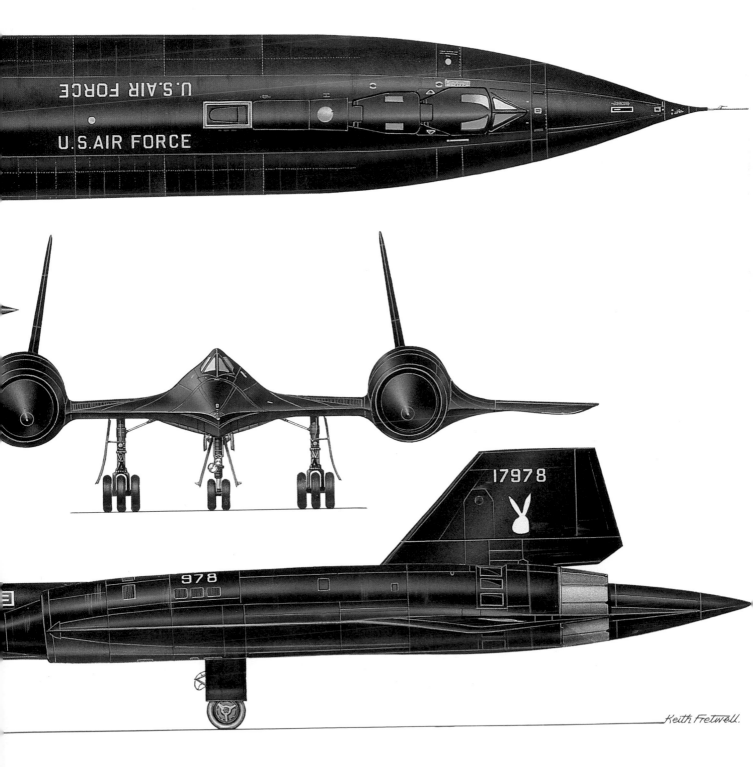

Keith Fretwell.

A-12 had largely remained an experimental aircraft, and throughout its early career had shown many weaknesses that could only be rectified by redesign. Ordered in late 1962, the SR-71A was the result. Externally very similar to the A-12, the SR-71 represented the definitive expression of the concept, with many small yet important changes to the A-12 design. It was bigger and heavier, with greater range and the ability to carry new and large sensors being developed for the CIA. Noticeable differences included a wider nose profile and an extended tailcone. Above all, the SR-71 incorporated the second cockpit of the YF-12A, allowing the carriage of a Reconnaissance Systems Officer to considerably cut the workload of the hard-pressed pilot.

First flight occurred on 22 December 1964 at Palmdale, and just over a year later, on 7 January 1966, the first example was handed over to the USAF's 4200th Strategic Reconnaissance Wing at Beale AFB. Reorganized later that year as the 9th SRW, this unit took the SR-71A into operations immediately and the improvement in capability over the A-12 was readily apparent.

'Super snooper'

Another programme of equal importance to the United States' intelligence gathering effort was also underway during the early 1960s in the altogether less glamorous field of Sigint. As recounted, the majority of these missions had been performed by the specially-configured Boeing B-47 Stratojets of the 55th SRW, but these aircraft, although much-loved by their crews, were short on capacity and comfort. The introduction into service of the Boeing KC-135 Stratotanker inflight-refueller and its C-135 transport derivative provided the intelligence community with a large, capacious jet aircraft with adequate range for the peripheral Sigint mission. First modifications were sponsored by the CIA under the codenames *Iron Lung* and *Briar Patch*, these referring to a KC-135A configured for intelligence gathering, with a capsule packed with listening gear towed behind the aircraft on a 12,000 ft (3660 m) cable. Three or four Ravens sat in the cabin monitoring instruments and recording intercepts of hostile emissions. Little is known of these early operations, but the individual air-

Continual improvements to the internal fit and continual evaluation of radical new equipment have kept the RC-135 fleet abreast of Soviet advances throughout its service career. Refinement to the RC-135C following special missions led to this, the first RC-135U.

craft underwent many transformations as new and more capable sensor systems were tested.

Having proved the worth of the C-135 airframe as an electronic eavesdropper more permanent modifications were undertaken, the first of them being designated RC-135D. These aircraft were allocated to the 6th Strategic Wing based at Eielson AFB in Alaska, from where they could keep watch on the eastern fringes of the Soviet Union, particularly the area around the Sea of Okhotsk, where Soviet ICBM tests were targetted from the launch sites around the Aral Sea and the southern Urals. As well as carrying an extensive suite of Sigint equipment, the RC-135D also possessed side-looking airborne radars in cylindrical fairings which extended forward from each wing root. Another recognition feature was a giant 'thimble' fairing on the nose which covered a further radar array, and which has become the trademark of the RC-135 family.

Unlucky 'Lisa Ann'

The 6th SW at Eielson was further augmented in 1969 by the introduction of the single RC-135E, which featured a giant radar in the forward fuselage, surrounded by a wrap-round dielectric radome which followed the original contours of the C-135 fuselage. In addition, the familiar 'thimble' nose was fitted and two equipment pods

were slung under the inboard wing sections. Once again, little is known of the operations of the RC-135E, but its service life was extremely short. A structural failure of the radome led to the aircraft crashing in the Bering Strait during 1969, with the tragic loss of all the crew on board.

Update for the 55th

Still persevering with the cramped and cold RB-47s, the 55th SRW had to wait until 1967 for their new aircraft, which arrived in the shape of the RC-135C *Big Team*. Originally delivered to the Air Force in 1964-65, the aircraft were immediately diverted to Martin at Baltimore for refit. When they returned to Offutt for operations they featured large cheek SLAR fairings and wingtip HF probes. Other sensors included a vertical camera in what had been the boom fairing of the tanker, and a comprehensive and highly capable Sigint suite. At the heart of this lay the AN/ASD-1 automatic reconnaissance unit and the QRC-259 superheterodyne receiver. Fitted with many other intercept receivers, direction finders and pulse analysers, the RC-135Cs were the most capable Sigint aircraft aloft, and represented a quantum leap over their RB-47 forebears. Vast improvements

Below left: Lifting off in a pall of smoke from the J57 turbojets, this aircraft is an RC-135D of the 6th Strategic Wing, normally based in Alaska. The cylindrical fairing on the fuselage hides a SLAR.

The 55th SRW moved to Offutt to receive its RC-135C 'Big Team' aircraft, and when these arrived they represented a huge leap in capability and comfort over the RB-47H. Chief feature of the new type was the cheek SLAR fairing.

Spyplane

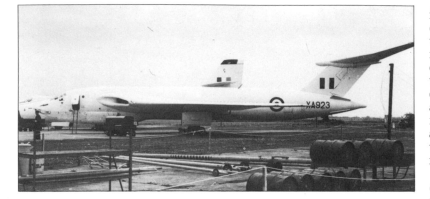

While No 543 Sqn waited for definitive Handley Page Victor SR.Mk 2s, the radar reconniassance role was handled by converted Victor B.Mk 1s such as this aircraft. Note the Valiant B(PR).Mk 1 in the background.

Right: Many Taiwanese U-2s suffered at the hands of Communist Chinese missiles while overflying the mainland. Most were U-2Cs, and most employed on monitoring the Communist ICBM programme.

Below: Sweden operated a small Sigint effort throughout the Baltic Sea, at first using Douglas Dakotas and then this Vickers Varsity, festooned with antennae.

were felt in other areas too: although the cabin of the RC-135 was crowded with electronic equipment of all kinds, the Ravens had individual consoles with desk-type stations, there was a rest area and the operators could stand up and walk around. Even extending one's legs had been unheard of in the belly of an RB-47. Inflight-refuelling was also possible, allowing an RC-135C to stay on station for as long as it was required, relief flight crews being carried. Other luxuries included the ability to carry technicians who could maintain and service the highly sensitive equipment in flight. Spare capacity allowed the RC-135C to serve as a test bed for new equipment while on operational missions, and the large cargo door in the port side, inherited from its tanker/transport forebear, allowed the cabin to be reconfigured for various mission requirements with the minimum of delay or fuss.

On arrival in service the RC-135C rapidly displaced the RB-47, and in so doing picked up the responsibility for providing the United States (and its most trusted Western allies) with the lion's share of its aerial strategic intelligence. Defences had become so capable that the peripheral Sigint mission was now the prime means of strategic reconnaissance, and no aircraft could undertake the role better than the RC-135.

V-bomber contribution

Throughout the 1960s other agencies were as much involved with strategic reconnaissance as was the US Air Force, particularly the air forces of the United Kingdom, Sweden and the Soviet Union. As well as No. 51 Sqn's Comets and Canberras, the RAF also introduced the Handley Page Victor SR.Mk 2 with No. 543 Sqn, these taking over the strategic reconnaissance role from the Valiants, which were grounded due to fatigue troubles. The Victors continued to map Soviet defences to provide ingress and egress information should Britain's V-bomber force need to attack the Soviet Union, but the emphasis shifted to long-range radar reconnaissance of the United Kingdom's maritime approaches. Pending introduction of the Victor SR.Mk 2 in December 1965, No. 543 Sqn at its Wyton base had bridged the gap after the demise of the Valiants with Victor B.Mk 1 bombers converted to the reconnaissance role. Towards the end of the decade the 'hot' areas of the globe were regularly criss-crossed by a plethora of converted transports, bombers and patrol aircraft, all packed with electronic equipment to record and analyse radar, communications and other electromagnetic emissions. There had been fewer incidents than during the preceding decade, largely due to the fact that the 'ferret' mission had become too dangerous, but some notable shoot-downs had occurred. By far the majority of incidents had involved the CIA/Nationalist Chinese U-2s which were still operating widely over mainland China, and paying the price. Another shoot-down involved a Douglas RB-66C (similar to the A-3 used by the US Navy) which, although normally used for operations of a more tactical

Devoid of marks, this is one of the Lockheed Constellations employed by the US Navy on eavesdropping flights in both East and West. The plethora of small aerials served an onboard Elint and Comint suite which was manned by large numbers of operators, language specialists and analysts. One of these was to be cruelly shot down by the North Koreans with the loss of 31 lives.

nature, was shot down by MiG fighters some 16 miles (25 km) inside East Germany during March 1964. Much speculation abounded at the time as to its true purpose: perhaps it was coincidence that a US satellite was orbiting above that part of Europe as the aircraft made its 'unintentional' incursion into WarPac airspace.

Act of vengeance

As the decade drew to a close the North Koreans perpetrated the worst act of aggression against a reconnaissance aircraft. North Korea had long been an area of particular interest to the United States and its fleet of strategic reconnaissance aircraft. Indeed, in 1965 a Boeing ERB-47H had been attacked unsuccessfully by North Korean fighters,

supposedly over international waters. However, on 16 April 1969, some fifteen months after the Korean attack on the spyship USS *Pueblo*, a Lockheed EC-121M Constellation of the US Navy's Pacific Fleet Reconnaissance Squadron, VQ-1, was attacked by two MiG-21s and shot down, with the loss of all 31 men on board. The EC-121 was a large and lumbering aircraft, with no hope of evading the MiGs despite receiving a warning from ground stations. The US aircraft was some 75 miles (120 km) from the North Korean coast and had only been 5 miles (8 km) closer during the course of its mission. Despite the flagrant flouting of international law by the Koreans, the only result was that in future all US flights in the region would be escorted by fighters.

Depite the lack of markings, it is known that this EC-121K Constellation served with VQ-2, the Atlantic Fleet Reconnaissance Squadron. Flying from bases mainly in the Mediterranean, this unit probed around the southern Soviet Union, while flying from further north in Europe allowed the EC-121s access to the Baltic and North Cape.

The Spyplane Goes to War

Strategic reconnaissance aircraft are usually involved with peacetime operations, but during wartime they have an important part to play, providing data for ground commanders unmatched by that produced by tactical assets. United States aircraft monitored Middle East skirmishes, while the vast array of reconnaissance assets were committed on a large scale to the war in Southeast Asia. Here their often overlooked activities are described, and the effect on the war effort.

Left: USAF SR-71As were involved in monitoring wars in both the Middle East and Southeast Asia. At immense altitude and speed, the 'Blackbird' could survey warzones without hindrance, with cameras, SLARs, infrared detectors and Sigint equipment scanning large areas with a single pass.

The U-2R version of the famous reconnaissance platform served the USAF well in the Middle East, being used on missions to verify ceasefire lines following the Yom Kippur war of 1973. Missions were usually launched from the secret RAF base at Akrotiri on Cyprus.

Although thought of mainly as a peacetime operation, the task of strategic reconnaissance has great application during wartime. Sigint aircraft operating over Korea had helped ground commanders pinpoint the radars which directed the deadly MiG-15 fighters against their strike aircraft. However, it was during the 1960s and early 1970s that the strategic reconnaissance aircraft went to war in earnest, in the Indian sub-continent, the Middle East and, above all, South East Asia.

As recounted earlier, Pakistani RB-57F high-altitude reconnaissance aircraft were highly active over India, and the intelligence gathered obviously served the Pakistanis well during the war with India in 1965. In the Middle East the United States was anxious to

keep a close watch on events, particularly during the two wars in 1967 and 1973 between Israel and its neighbours. Although U-2s are known to have made several flights in the war zone in 1970, it seems likely that American aircraft kept watch during the days of conflict in both wars. Certainly, in 1973 Lockheed SR-71s made several overflights of Egypt and Syria, drawing complaints of airspace violations from Egypt. There is much to suggest that the intelligence gleaned by these flights was handed directly to the Israeli high command, for their winning military move on 14 October, exposing a weak point in the Egyptian defences, followed one day after a double SR-71 overflight of Egyptian lines. Towards the end of the war, Mikoyan-Gurevich MiG-25R high-

Right: A U-2R leaves the runway at Akrotiri on a long mission over the Middle East. The open camera ports in the Q-bay and nose cone leave no doubt as to the nature of the mission; to survey military installations in the area.

Right: A U-2R leaves the runway at Akrotiri on a long mission over the Middle East. The open camera ports in the Q-bay and nose cone leave no doubt as to the nature of the mission; to survey military installations in the area.

Left: The French introduced Sigint to Southeast Asia during the later years of their involvement in Indo-China. Eavesdropping equipment was fitted into Nord NC.701 Martinets or Beech C-45s, the operators listening in to Viet Minh communications and pinpointing the positions of the transmitters. Such equipment was of World War II vintage.

Below: To prove that the strategic reconnaissance aircraft got embroiled in war is this picture of a 55th SRW ERB-47H at Tan Son Nhut in South Vietnam, awaiting a mission while an installation burns in the background following a Viet Cong mortar strike. RB-47s flew 'Box Top' Sigint missions, and 'United Effort' missions in conjunction with drones.

altitude reconnaissance aircraft flown by Soviet pilots began operations from Egypt, but their deployment was short. Both Israel and Egypt agreed to American reconnaissance aircraft being the vehicle to monitor the truce that followed the end of hostilities.

Vietnam war

South East Asia saw the greatest application of Cold War reconnaissance techniques to a 'hot' war, with all branches of the US intelligence community taking part in the battle against the North Vietnamese and the Viet Cong guerrillas. The first use of electronic listening devices in the theatre had been carried out by French forces during the Indochina war of the early 1950s, when they were fighting the Viet Minh. Rudimentary Comint and direction finding equipment was carried aloft in aircraft such as the Nord N.C.701 Martinet, to eavesdrop on Viet Minh communications to aid ground commanders, and this basic task was carried on by the United States as they began their embroilment in the conflict during the early 1960s. As the war progressed, and as the North Vietnamese received ever more sophisticated equipment from the Soviet Union and China, so the Sigint effort was stepped up by the United States.

Small beginnings

Before the war Vietnam had occupied only a small part of the overall US reconnaissance effort. Boeing RB-47H Stratojets of the 55th SRW patrolled the coastline at regular intervals from their base at Yokota in Japan, but these flights were unproductive as the Vietnamese possessed little in the way of radar, and the presence of Communist China to the

Fetching up in the warzone from time to time were the RC-135Cs of the 55th SRW, which provided their unique contribution to the war effort while maintaining their global commitments. This view shows amply why the C-model received the nickname 'Chipmunk'.

Below right: Taxiing at Kadena is a RC-135M 'Combat Apple'. From the clean state of the airframe it can be deduced that this example has just returned from refit in the States.

Below: Orbits were flown for 12 hours at a time, only stopping when the relief aircraft arrived on station. Photographed from another RC-135M, this aircraft turns for home after its stint. The patches on the skin are testament to the hammering the aircraft received during the Southeast Asia war.

north was a far more attractive proposition to the Ravens crammed into their converted bomb bay. By 1964, however, the conflict in South East Asia was beginning to snowball and more time was spent in the combat zone, the RB-47s now flying from Kadena AB on Okinawa. This was because their Yokota base had been deemed politically unacceptable following local protests against the use of a Japanese base for U-2 and RB-47 flights. In addition to regular Sigint patrols in the Gulf of Tonkin, the RB-47s were also involved with *United Effort* missions in support of drone operations, of which more later.

'Combat Apple'

As the RB-47H was being phased out of the inventory, so the Boeing RC-135 picked up more of its missions. Based at Yokota (before the local opposition became too vociferous) were the RC-135M aircraft of the 82nd Strategic Reconnaissance Squadron, who were largely tasked against Chinese and eastern Soviet targets, particularly in the Petro-

pavlovsk region. The RC-135M was a relatively inconspicuous modification of the C-135B transport with the familiar 'thimble' nose and teardrop fairings on the rear fuselage. Carrying a full complement of Ravens, the RC-135M was soon providing 24-hour coverage of the South East Asia war zone from Kadena. Each mission lasted around 19 hours (with 12 on station) before being relieved by another aircraft. These *Combat Apple* missions were the single most important Sigint flights undertaken during the war, providing Elint information on North Vietnamese radars, Comint, warning of MiG flights and SAM launches, and control and co-ordination of rescue attempts. In addition to this monumental tasking, the 82nd SRS was still flying all its Sino-Soviet missions. Only six aircraft were available for this, and the heavy flying schedule played havoc with their airframes, particularly as they were expected to fly in the worst weather that the South East Asia hothouse could throw at them. Inevitably aircraft had to return to the States for overhaul, and while one was away an RC-135D was diverted from the 6th SW in Alaska to help out on *Combat Apple* missions; used to the dry cold of Alaska, these aircraft proved extremely difficult to operate in the hot and humid climate. Other problems arose from the lack of range and power experienced in this version, as it was powered by J57 turbojets rather than the

TF33 turbofans of the RC-135M.

Combat Apple missions were initially flown over the Gulf of Tonkin, aircraft flying a wide orbit in the Gulf and stopping to fly tighter orbits if an area of interest was found. MiG fighters sometimes attempted to intercept the heavily-laden RC-135s but these were unsuccessful. Nevertheless, the threat was enough for the US Navy to provide a fighter escort for *Combat Apple* operations from its carriers sailing in the Gulf. As the war progressed a further operating area was allocated, that being over northern Laos. This added flight time to the mission, but allowed the sensitive receivers of the RC-135M to gain access to a large part of North Vietnam.

Specialist versions

Other members of the RC-135 family were involved in the war in South East Asia. The first C-135 to be employed on reconnaissance tasks was still on the inventory, and still used for various test and special missions. Designated KC-135R, this aircraft and a companion fetched up in the war zone whenever a special mission was required, and were regularly reconfigured to cope with new equipment. These aircraft were often tasked against a specific target and their mission routing reflected this, tight orbits being performed in a particular area of interest. RC-

135Cs of the 55th SRW also made regular visits to the combat zone, although these were mainly part of the C-model's global commitments. Indeed, the capabilities of the RC-135C were such that it needed only a short time in the war zone to analyse and record its targets. Due to the delay in its introduction into service, the RC-135C could not be spared for special missions in South East Asia until around 1970, by which time it could pick up some of the missions of the KC-135Rs. Some of these special missions led to the RC-135U *Combat Sent*, which was a converted RC-135C with vastly improved equipment fits. Capabilities of this new version remain highly classified, but have been described as 'science fiction'. Initially externally similar to the RC-135C, the 'U-bird' later sprouted enormous SLAR fairings on the cheeks, with large 'rabbit's ear' antennae above the SLARs, fin-top, tailcone and wingtip fairings. With the RC-135C and RC-135U

Above: RC-135Cs often carried special equipment in addition to their regular reconnaissance fit. These 'specials' led to the RC-135U 'Combat Sent', the first incarnation of which is seen here visiting the warzone.

Above left: Touching down on Kadena's runway is the KC-135R which was used initially for experimental missions. As the RC-135C caught up with its taskings, it replaced the KC-135R on the trials flights, releasing it for training purposes.

The definitive RC-135U configuration included huge SLAR/Elint fairings, forward-facing chin radome and 'rabbit's ear' antennae above the SLAR. Other antennae were located in the boom fairing, tailcone, fintip and wingtips.

Left: Characterised by the cylindrical SLAR fairing, the RC-135D occasionally helped out on 'Combat Apple' missions.

Above: RC-135U at Kadena. The large crew entered the aircraft through the open hatch and ladderway.

Protected by blast revetments, the 'Combat Apple fleet of the 376th Strategic Wing line up at Kadena. Visible are two RC-135Ms, an RC-135D and an RC-135C on the far end.

picking up the special missions, the two KC-135Rs were released to training duties with the 376th SW at Kadena and the 55th SRW at Offutt.

Electronic variations

Of course the RB-47s and RC-135s were by no means the only Sigint aircraft operational in South East Asia. A large number of types were employed on varying duties, from the giant Constellation to the diminutive Beaver.

The US Navy ably assisted the RC-135s on eavesdropping missions with VQ-1's fleet of snoopers. Lockheed EC-121Ks and EC-121Ms were regular visitors to the war zone, flying from both their home base at Atsugi in Japan and from forward bases such as Da Nang in South Vietnam. Carrying huge crews, the EC-121s patrolled the Gulf of Tonkin in addition to their peacetime missions aimed at Korea, China and the eastern seaboard of the Soviet Union. Flying along-

Left: This rare photograph shows one of the Elint consoles aboard an RC-135M during 'Combat Apple' operations. A considerable improvement over the RB-47Hs, the RC-135 offered the 'Crow' a comfortable seat, a table to work on and modern instruments, many of them automated. Among the 'black boxes' are several oscilloscopes to display wave patterns and pulse repetition information. Several such stations are ranged down the side of the RC-135.

Right: Augmenting the specialists on electronic intelligence missions were several aircraft that were tailored to more tactical requirements. Among them was the Douglas EB-66 (previously RB-66) Destroyer, which was primarily concerned with ECM protection of strike aircraft, but also provided intelligence on North Vietnamese radars for strategic consumption.

Above: Seen Stateside, this pair of snoopers formed the basic US Navy contribution to Sigint during the war. Leading is the Lockheed EC-121 while following is the Douglas EA-3B.

Above: Sweeping in across the ramp, a VQ-1 Douglas EA-3B lands on a carrier. Noticeable on the starboard side are windows, which illuminate the cabin for the equipment operators.

side them on these missions were the Douglas EA-3B Skywarriors, which operated from Da Nang and from carriers operating in the Gulf. As the war entered the 1970s, so the Lockheed EP-3B electronic eavesdropping version of the Orion maritime patroller began

to pick up the missions of the elderly EC-121s, which were then retired after many years of sterling service.

Tactical Comint

Battlefield eavesdropping became a regular feature during the war in South East Asia. Both the US Army and Air Force were involved in this, flying aircraft on orbits to pinpoint Communist positions. Chief type for the Air Force was the Douglas EC-47, various versions of which were packed with direction finding gear and Vietnamese language specialists. Immediate battle plans could be ascertained, and the position of transmitting Communist radios fixed for attack by other forces. The Army was heavily involved in this mission, flying many different types. Most important amongst these were various versions of the Beech King Air with RU-21 designations. Other types were the de Havil-

Left: The Marine Corps also flew electronic intelligence missions in Vietnam, using the elderly Douglas EF-10B Skyknight with VMCJ-1. It was more usually employed on ECM protection.

Below: Caught during a stop at Da Nang, South Vietnam, is this VQ-1 Lockheed EC-121, named 'Miss Philippines'. The Constellations flew Sigint missions around North Vietnam in addition to their peacetime Sino-Soviet tasks.

Above: EA-3Bs operated from both carriers and Da Nang (illustrated) on Sigint missions. The 'PR' tailcode led VQ-1 to adopt the callsign 'Peter Rabbit'.

Below: Replacing the EC-121 with VQ-1 during the later years of the war was the Lockheed EP-3B Orion, inheriting much of the systems from its predecessor.

Spyplane

Left: Intended primarily as an ECM platform, the Grumman EA-6A supplanted the EF-10B with VMCJ-1. Like its predecesor, the EA-6A found time to perform some Elint flights.

Right: Tactical Photint types, led by the McDonnell RF-101C Voodoo, overflew North Vietnam to provide coverage of strategic targets during the early years. The 'long bird' was extremely tough and fast, attributes well appreciated by reconnaissance crews.

Below: Battlefield Comint was the tasking of many small aircraft, chiefly operated by the US Army. Primary type was the Beech RU-21, identified by large dipole antennae on the wings.

Above: Aiding the Army types on battlefield Comint duties were a handful of Air Force EC-47s, operating under the 'Hawk Eye' codename. Several versions were used.

land Canada RU-1 Otter and RU-6 Beaver, the Grumman OV-1 Mohawk and the Beech RU-8 Seminole. Most of these missions were flown over South Vietnam, although the Air Force's EC-47s were particularly active over Laos. Largest of the aircraft operated by the Army was the Lockheed Neptune, which was flown by the 1st Radio Research Company and made regular missions over South Viet-

nam. Designated RP-2E (sometimes AP-2E), these aircraft were involved in similar work to their smaller brethren but carried considerably more refined and sensitive equipment.

High fliers

Sigint gathering by converted transports and maritime patrollers had been undertaken on an unprecedented scale during the war in

South East Asia, but no less important to the war effort was the contribution of SAC's high-fliers, the Lockheed U-2 and SR-71. March 1964 saw the first deployment of the U-2 to this theatre when U-2C aircraft of the 4080th SRW moved to Bien Hoa to begin combat operations. Initial reconnaissance assets in the region largely rested upon the McDonnell RF-101C Voodoo, but this had severe shortcomings in the type of sensors it could carry and the areas over which it could fly. The U-2 quickly filled the gap. Carrying both optical and electronic sensors, the U-2s not only made reconnaissance flights around North Vietnam's borders, but also over the country itself to help prepare United States forces for attacks against the North. During late 1964 the *Dragon Lady* U-2s at Bien Hoa adopted the flat-black colour scheme that

had characterized the aircraft of the CIA.

Early missions involved overflights of North Vietnam, but the adoption of the SA-2 surface-to-air missile led to a curtailment of these. The overflight mission was largely en-

Above: Caught by his wingman, this RF-101C flies a high-level photo-run over Kep airfield near Hanoi. In revetments on the airfield are North Vietnamese MiGs.

Left: Battlefield reconnaissance sometimes involved electronic techniques, and the prime exponent was the Grumman OV-1 Mohawk, equipped with a pod-mounted SLAR. Other Mohawks carried Sigint gear.

Right: Maintenance men swarm over a U-2 after its landing at Bien Hoa following a Southeast Asia sortie. The aircraft is one of two which featured 'ram's horn' antennae on the rear fuselage, presumably for Elint work. The pair were originally U-2Fs, complete with air refuelling receptacles.

Spyplane

The initial variant of 'Dragon Lady' employed in Southeast Asia was the U-2C, this example sporting slipper tanks on the wing to extend range. This aircraft has the distinction of being the first Air Force U-2 to have an all-black paint scheme.

Above: The advent of the U-2R introduced greater sensor payload to the U-2's taskings, together with greater safety and comfort for the pilot.

Owing to the long endurance of the type, the U-2R was widely used for Comint, and as such carried a wide array of antennae to record communications. Such fits were a common sight at U-Tapao, where this U-2R drifts back in to land.

trusted to the nascent drone operation (also conducted by the 4080th SRW), while the U-2s took to peripheral missions which came increasingly to rely on electronic sensors. Two aircraft, which had earlier been U-2Fs with inflight-refuelling capability, appeared in Vietnam with giant 'ram's horn' antennae sprouting from the rear fuselage. For the U-2 community the Vietnam operations were extremely different from those undertaken earlier. Gone were the days of secrecy around the base, and crews could park their 'craft in the open, file flight plans and talk on the

radio. However, the navigation aids during the early days in Vietnam were extremely primitive.

New 'Dragon Lady'

In February 1966 the 4080th SRW was redesignated as the 100th SRW, and the U-2 squadron became the 349th SRS. As the decade ended a vast improvement came in the shape of the U-2R, a completely redesigned aircraft which was larger in all dimensions and capable of carrying a much greater sensor payload. Safety during landing was increased, this being a problem which had dogged the early versions of the U-2 throughout its career. During 1970 the Vietnam deployment achieved full squadron status as the 99th SRS and moved to U-Tapao RTNAF in Thailand, from where it continued its operations around the peripheries of North Vietnam. By now the missions were almost entirely of a Sigint nature. Chief discipline undertaken by the U-2Rs was Comint. Blessed with a phenomenal endurance and altitude, the U-2R could cruise for hours while lapping up any communications beneath it. Many of the aircraft seen at U-Tapao during this period featured large paddle-shaped ae-

A U-2R prepares to lauch from U-Tapao, with paddle aerials under the wings. Considerable wing flex denotes a full fuel load, necessary for the 12 hour mission that lay ahead.

rials under the wing. Attention also shifted towards China, where *Senior Book* missions were aimed to collect Comint with the aid of drones. Other important tasks undertaken during this period included preparation and assessment of the *Linebacker II* bombing raids of December 1972. Despite the return of the majority of USAF assets in the theatre to the United States, the U-2Rs stayed on at U-Tapao until early 1976, their mission requirements increasing as the war drew to a close with the unit setting enviable records of safe operations against both China and the now united Vietnam.

'Habu' joins the war

Also active in the upper atmosphere above Vietnam was the Lockheed SR-71A, flying from the Okinawa base of Kadena. Under the codename *Giant Scale* the SR-71s flew regular Photint missions over the war zone, with a secondary Sigint tasking. Washington regularly denied the existence of the Okinawa detachment, but it was hard to conceal the Mach 3 'Blackbird' which shook the island as it roared off on another mission; this caused minor traffic jams on the public road which passed the runway as drivers stopped to marvel at the beast. It was on Okinawa that the SR-71 picked up its nickname 'Habu', the aircraft said to resemble the Habu pit viper which inhabited the Pacific island. The SR-71 missions over Vietnam were flown in conjunction with others over Korea, and around China and the Soviet Union, and the 'Blackbird' had its own special fleet of Boeing KC-135Q tankers stationed at Kadena to refuel it

A U-2R prepares to lauch from U-Tapao, with paddle aerials under the wings. Considerable wing flex denotes a full fuel load, necessary for the 12 hour mission that lay ahead.

Above: This remarkable sequence shows a SA-2 'Guideline' missile tracking a U-2 over North Vietnam. The missile exploded close but harmlessly beneath the aircraft.

Below: 100th SRW U-2Rs flew from U-Tapao until 1976, housed in these giant hangars. The yellow structure in the foreground protected the pilot from the sun or rain while he ingressed the aircraft.

Spyplane

Above: High over the South China Sea, a Lockheed SR-71 from Kadena slides underneath a KC-135Q tanker for refuelling. SR-71 missions were targetted against Vietnamese, Chinese and Korean targets.

leased about possible mid-1960s use from Kadena of the SR-71's A-12 predecessor.

At times maligned and ridiculed, one reconnaissance programme in South East Asia gained more fame than any other and its importance to the war effort appears paramount. Despite the heroics and achievements of the RC-135s, U-2s and SR-71s, it was the unmanned aircraft which gained the fame. The attractions of pilotless aircraft had long interested the US Air Force, yet the only serious attempts to provide such a vehicle had occurred during World War II and the Korean War, when standard aircraft were packed with explosives and remotely controlled on to their chosen targets. It was to be the loss of the U-2 over Cuba which jarred the Air Force into resurrecting the drone programme for reconnaissance purposes. Ryan's Firebee I drone was the vehicle chosen for adaptation, and by 1964 the little aircraft were ready for operational evaluation. As the Cuban situation had long cooled, the 'Bugs' were sent to Kadena to fly against North Korea and China. War in Vietnam was escalating, so the drone operations of the 4080th SRW were hastily sent to Bien Hoa AB in South Vietnam. After a brief return to Kadena, the Bien Hoa detachment was ready to begin combat operations by October 1964.

Hercules mother ship

These operations called for the 'Bug' to be launched from a Lockheed DC-130 Hercules mother ship, which carried the drones on large pylons mounted under the wing. Drones were programmed on the ground with a flight plan that was checked by the Launch Control Officer carried in the Hercules, and inside of which was a plethora of equipment to launch, control and track the RPVs throughout their flight. Immediately before launch, the LCO started the engines,

during missions. Little has been released about the SR-71's operations during the war years, but it seems certain that their unique photographic capabilities would have aided the American commanders greatly in assessing North Vietnamese defences and for the planning of US raids. Even less has been re-

Left: Okinawa was regularly hit by violent storms and most aircraft moved out until they had passed. The SR-71s stayed however, and this one came to grief during a landing in strong crosswinds.

Below: An SR-71A taxis in post-mission past a row of RC-135s at Kadena. Both types operated under a cloak of secrecy throughout the conflict, and also had pressing taskings elsewhere in the region.

The Spyplane Goes to War

Above: The SR-71 picked up its 'Habu' nickname while operating on Okinawa, the local inhabitants likening it to a local species of poisonous snake.

Right: SR-71s have rarely carried markings other than official ones, yet this aircraft (64-17974) carried these 'Habu' mission marks, together with the name 'Ichi Ban'.

checked their power setting and monitored the drone's systems, before it was dropped from the pylon and allowed to carry out its mission, closely monitored by two officers on board the DC-130. A simple onboard computer system allied to a variety of navigation systems flew the reconnaissance vehicle to its intended target and then on to the recovery area.

Once guided into the recovery area by a ground-based Drone Recovery Officer, the drone shut down its engine and deployed a drogue 'chute, which in turn deployed a main 'chute under which the 'Bug' hung as the recovery team moved in. This consisted of a Sikorsky CH-3 helicopter with a grapnel and cable suspended between two poles under the rear fuselage. As the drone floated earthwards the CH-3 manoeuvred in to snag the small drogue chute. As it was snatched, the main chute was discarded and the helicopter attempted to stop the drone's descent. Being heavy vehicles this involved paying out cable under tension and gradually breaking the fall of the drone until it was suspended on a large length of cable. This cable was slowly reeled in until the drone was happily carried underneath the CH-3, trailing a small drogue 'chute to stop it swinging beneath the helicopter. It was then transported back to the recovery base for reuse. Inevitably, some drones 'got away' during recovery. Some were missed by the helicopter and floated to an unceremonious landing, others did not shut down their engines and flew on until they crashed. Many of these runaways lived to fight another day. Nevertheless, the helicopter crews returned a 96.7 per cent recovery rate throughout the Vietnam war.

Many versions of drone existed and were

used on just about every conceivable reconnaissance task. Cameras and Sigint sensors formed a large part of the payload, but other systems that were carried included real-time TV cameras with a datalink back to the DC-130. Versions of the basic Ryan 147 (AQM-34) drone stretched from low-altitude models with a 13 ft (3.96 m) span to the high-altitude AQM-34Q and R models with 32 ft (9.75 m) wings. Some had underwing fuel tanks to increase range and most were equipped with some form of defensive electronics. Among these were a SAM jammer and a system to warn of impending fighter attack and initiate evasive manoeuvres. Others tested the HIDE system which reduced radar reflectivity ('stealth' techniques) and the HAT-RAC high-altitude evasion system.

Initial missions were largely flown against the SA-2 missile system under the *United Effort* programme. This involved a drone equipped with a travelling wave tube, which

Above: This is the Launch Control Officer position on board the DC-130 Hercules motherplane. From here the drone's engines were started and systems checked, after which the 'Bug' was launched.

Below left: Once in the correct area, the drone deployed a large main chute to slow its descent, and a smaller drogue chute which the helicopter aimed for during recovery.

Below: The Lockheed DC-130E was the definitive mother-ship, with pylons for two drones. The nose blister housed a microwave guidance system for drone control.

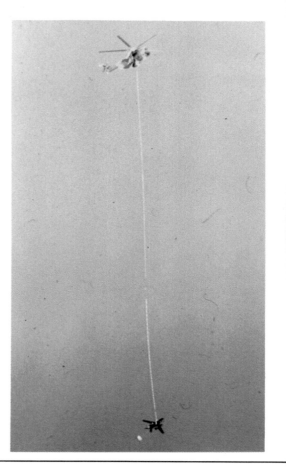

A small drogue chute was deployed from the rear of the drone to avoid it swinging about underneath the helicopter during the transit back to base. The helicopter is the Sikorsky CH-3E and the drone an AQM-34R high-altitude model.

Far right: This CH-3E has just trapped the drone and is about to reel in the cable to bring it under control.

gave it a similar radar return to a U-2, flying over areas known to be defended by SA-2 missiles. When fired at the guidance and fusing data of the missile was transmitted by the drone to a Boeing RB-47H orbiting away from the area. After several abortive attempts the *United Effort* team finally got it right, providing the United States with some of the most valuable Elint data it had ever received, allowing countermeasures to be quickly evolved against the SAM menace. However, by far the most important task of the drones

AQM-34 in operation

Although the 'Bugs' performed many different missions, the sorties were all flown in a similar way, and this is described in this series of drawings. Not all drones were caught by the helicopter, but many of these crash-landed without fatal damage in paddyfields and the sea, and were soon back in action.

Take-off
Prior to take-off, the LCOs programme the flight plan into the drone. The DC-130 then heads for the launch point with its precious cargo, the LCOs performing pre-flight checks as they transit

The launch
When at the launch area, the LCOs fire up the 'bug's' engine and it falls away from the Hercules to begin its flight. Control of the drone is handed over to the ARCOs

The missions

AQM-34H
This was the Project 'Litterbug' model, used to drop propaganda leaflets over the North. Some aircraft operated without the wing pods

AQM-34M
A low-altitude photo-recon model ('Buffalo Hunter') with improved nav systems over the L, the AQM-34M(L) was further modified to carry Loran gear. It had the best launch/return ratio of any model – 97.3 per cent

AQM-34P
A high-altitude day photo model, t version introduced a new engine. Note the large-span wings for high level work

AQM-34Q (right)
Another high altitude model ('Combat Dawn'), this featured a new wing complete with external fuel tanks. Real-time sensors were carried

AQM-34L (above)
The L was the low-altitude workhorse, with over 1,600 launches. The high-time 'bugs' were all Ls (*Tomcat*, *Budweiser*, *Baby Buck* and *Ryan's Daughter*). The LTV version featured real-time television

AQM-34R
The definitive high-altitude type, refined from the Q-model with better reliability. It carried out the longest flight (7.8 hours by R8) and hit a 96.8 per cent launch/return ratio

Many of the drones outlived their expected service careers by some considerable time. Leading the way was AQM-34L 'Tom Cat' with 68 missions. The L-model was a low-altitude Photint drone, which performed the bulk of Southeast Asia missions.

was low-altitude Photint, and at this the 'Bugs' excelled. The workhorse of this role was the AQM-34L, a usual mission profile seeing the drone being launched over the Gulf of Tonkin, or perhaps over South Vietnam or Laos, from where it penetrated North Vietnamese airspace at low-level to avoid SAMs. After flying over its allotted series of targets it headed for the recovery area, climbing to high altitude once out of SAM range. Inevitably many drones were downed by North Vietnamese (and Chinese) defences during their missions, yet they provided an enormous amount of photographic and electronic intelligence that was vital to the war effort. In addition to the SA-2 intercept, other prime intelligence gained included photographic evidence of the first SA-2 missiles in North Vietnam, the first MiG-21 fighters and the presence of Soviet helicopters in the country. Their contribution during *Linebacker II* was enormous.

Low- and medium-altitude missions formed the staple diet of the 4080th/100th SRW drone operations, with just about every

kind of sensor that could be carried aloft, but these were by no means the only use of drones in South East Asia. *Combat Dawn* (largely Comint) missions at altitudes up to 65,000 ft (19810m) were flown over both North Vietnam and China during the later years of the war. The AQM-34Q and R drones used were aided by manned U-2Rs from U-

Below: The two squadrons of the 100th SRW co-operated closely on many missions, combining the talents of the U-2R and the drones. This drone is a low-altitude AQM-34M(L), the small blade antenna underneath serving a LORAN navigation system.

...covery

...one was directed towards the catch zone and, if all functioned properly, the engine cut out and the parachute recovery system deployed (1). ...ain chute opens and slows the aircraft down (2). The CH-3E has been orbiting in the area and moves in to make the catch. Two poles ...ed to the rear fuselage hold a wire between them, to which are attached the main cable and grapnel hooks. These grapnel hooks snag ...s small chute (3). The main chute is discarded, and the helo starts to take the weight of the drone. The helo pays out line until the drone ...alling away from the helo, and then slowly winches the cable in (4)

Safe return
The helo winches the drone in to a manageable position and heads for home (Da Nang or Nakhon Phanom). The helo deposits the drone gently back on to the ground, where the ground crew set about preparing it for transport back to the launch base (Bien Hoa or U-Tapao)

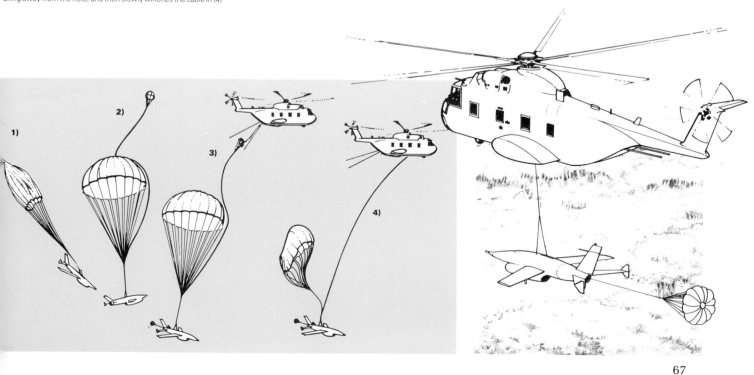

Left: It has never been released if there were launches of the D-21 drone in the Pacific theatre, but plenty of rumours abound. Launches were from a Boeing B-52H.

Above: Another successful catch by the helicopter crews, and another drone returned to fight another day. Recoveries were effected at Da Nang for most of the war.

Tapao, although much of the systems carried by both platforms were entirely automatic or ground-controlled. Many of these missions were launched from Osan AB in South Korea. During 1972 several drones were configured to drop leaflets as part of Operation 'Litterbug', while under codename *Belfry Express*, the US Navy operated ship-launched RPVs for a time. Other drones were tested with live armament, including Maverick missiles and Hobo TV-guided bombs. As recounted earlier, the Lockheed-developed Mach-4 D-21 drone may have been used operationally in South East Asia.

Drone achievements

In July 1970 the drone operations of the 350th SRS, 100th SRW moved to U-Tapao in Thailand, along with the same Wing's U-2 ops, and two years later the recovery group at Da Nang moved to Nakhon Phanom in Thailand. Many of the 'Bugs' racked up impressive individual tallies, led by the AQM-34L 'Tom Cat' with 68 sorties to its credit. Others took on identities in a way unmatched by piloted aircraft, showing

perhaps a propensity for ignoring all recovery instructions and insisting on a landing in water, or managing to return almost shot to pieces by North Vietnamese defences, to be lovingly decorated with a Purple Heart. One flew so low that it went under power cables and met a MiG fighter head-on over the runway at Kep, others returned trailing vast amounts of vegetation or cables. Several MiGs were lost by running out of fuel while chasing drones, or being shot down by other MiGs or friendly gunfire. On the reverse side, US Navy fighters accidentally shot down a number of drones after mistaking them for MiGs.

Throughout the drone operation in South East Asia, the 4080th/100th SRW met with nothing but success, yet the programme ground to a halt as the war ended with the last mission being flown on 30 April 1975, the date of the final panic-stricken evacuation from Saigon. Returning quietly to the States the drones and their mission were equally quietly mothballed; only in recent years has the full extent of their achievements come to light.

Right: Drones and SR-71s kept up a constant Photint effort over North Vietnam, allowing very little to escape the US intelligence community. Photographs such as this one, showing MiG-17s and -21s on Phuc Yen airfield, kept US commanders abreast of North Vietnamese advances, while helping them plan air strikes against such targets.

Below: DC-130s and a collection of high-altitude drones bask in the Southeast Asia sun, protected against sapper attacks by revetments. Only recently has the full extent of the drone's contribution become known, yet the whole operation subsided into nothing following the end of the war.

Reconnaissance Across the Globe

Left: The huge 'Hog' nose of a Boeing RC-135W nestles under the boom of a KC-135A tanker as it takes on fuel during a reconnaissance mission. The RC-135 fleet built on its already remarkable list of achievements throughout the 1970s, bringing its unique eavesdropping talents to new parts of the world such as the Middle East.

The 1970s saw a continued increase in the level of strategic reconnaissance activities around the globe, led as ever by the high-tech spyplanes of the United States and the majestic fleet of Soviet patrollers. An era of sensor development ensued, while many of the 1960s aircraft continued to provide the bulk of the missions. More importantly, the decade saw a dramatic proliferation of reconnaissance assets outside of the UK, US and USSR. European nations joined the ranks of strategic reconnaissance aircraft users, as did others elsewhere.

Having started late in the aerial espionage race, during the early 1960s the Soviet Union embarked with gusto on its own programmes, with the Tupolev 'Bears' and 'Badgers' leading the way out over the world's oceans as they set about cataloguing Western navies. NATO ships on exercises in international waters became more than accustomed to Soviet snoopers flying at low level over their vessels. The giant Tupolev Tu-95 'Bear' was the king of the Soviet reconnaissance craft; blessed with phenomenal range and endur-

ance it could reach out over the world's oceans so that no Western ships could escape its cameras and electronic sensors. Several versions have existed, the most common of which is 'Bear-D', a general purpose maritime reconnaissance, Sigint and missile targeting type, readily identified by the huge 'Big Bulge' search radar carried under its belly. This version, in service since 1965, has been the subject of most interceptions. Other important reconnaissance versions of the Soviet monster are the 'Bear-C', which is a

Below: 'Bear', 'Bison' and 'Badger' continued their flights around Western coasts and navies. British forces are as acquainted with the snoopers as anybody, illustrated by this Royal Navy Phantom shadowing a 'Bear-D'. The huge 'Big Bulge' belly radar is plainly obvious.

Tupolev Tu-95 'Bear-D'

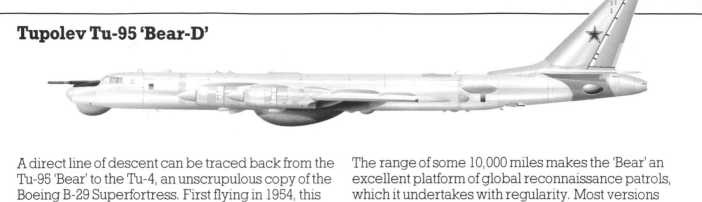

A direct line of descent can be traced back from the Tu-95 'Bear' to the Tu-4, an unscrupulous copy of the Boeing B-29 Superfortress. First flying in 1954, this giant is powered by four Kuznetsov turboprops generating some 12,000 ehp each, and driving massive contra-rotating propellers, creating enough noise to be heard inside intercepting aircraft.

The range of some 10,000 miles makes the 'Bear' an excellent platform of global reconnaissance patrols, which it undertakes with regularity. Most versions have been seen on 'ferret' missions, even the missile carriers having sufficient electronic equipment to carry out purely Sigint flights. The 'Bear' is still in limited production as the 'Bear-H' cruise missile carrier.

dedicated Elint type first seen in 1964, and the 'Bear-E' which carries six or seven massive cameras in the weapons bay. Often operating in concert with one of the Sigint types, the 'Bear-E' spends much of its operational missions photographing Western ships in minute detail as they sail in international waters, while the Sigint 'Bear' catalogues the ships' radars and communications systems.

Augmenting the 'Bears' on the massive Soviet maritime effort are two patrol versions of the Myasishchev Mya-4 'Bison' bomber.

'Bison-C' is the most capable, with a large search radar mounted in the nose and numerous Elint antennae placed around the aircraft. The third member of the maritime trio is the smaller Tupolev Tu-16 'Badger', which in its 'Badger-D, -F and -K' versions is a dedicated naval Elint platform. Without the range of the Tu-95 or Mya-4, the Tu-16 operates closer to the Soviet Union, but can extend its range by inflight-refuelling and is regularly seen, particularly in European waters.

Maritime reconnaissance remains the

A unit which intercepts Soviet aircraft regularly is the 57th Fighter Interceptor Squadron, based at Keflavik on Iceland. This self-portrait shows a 57th FIS pilot flying escort to a snooping 'Bear-D'.

Tupolev Tu-22 'Blinder-C'

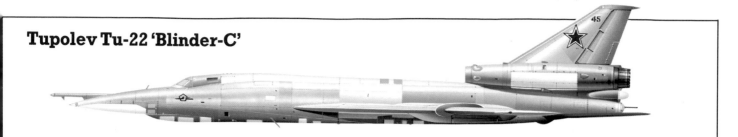

First noted in 1961, the Tu-22 is still in service as a missile carrier, but it has spawned one important reconnaissance variant, the 'Blinder-C'. This variant fills the weapons bay with various camera installations, while Elint equipment is located in other parts of the fuselage. Around 35 are in service, mostly flying over the Baltic and Black Seas, keeping watch over the maritime approaches to the Soviet Union. Although somewhat lacking in range, the type's high speed makes it a useful reconnaissance tool. It is augmented by the derived and more capable Tu-26 'Backfire', which carries reconnaissance gear on a bomb-bay pallet.

Above: 'Bear-C' was originally a missile carrier but has more recently turned to Sigint tasks. The plethora of onboard sensors can be augmented by equipment carried in wing pods, while some 'Bear-Cs' have a faired in tailcone with further listening gear.

Right: Occasionally seen in company with a 'Bear-C' or 'Bear-D' Sigint platform, the 'Bear-E' has Photint as its primary role. A battery of huge cameras is carried in the vacant weapons bay, peering through seven windows in the belly.

Below: Although small in number, the 'Bear-D' is commonly seen by Western fighters such as this VF-142 Grumman Tomcat. US carrier groups are a natural target for the 'Bear's' listening gear.

Spyplane

The huge wing of the Myasishchev Mya-4 was a major manufacturing feat for its day. Unable to reach its specified range, the Mya-4 bomber found employment elsewhere as a maritime and electronic reconnaissance platform. This is a 'Bison-C' with maritime nose radar.

Rare photograph of two Elint 'Bison-Bs' together escorted by US Navy Tomcats over the Atlantic. Some 'Bisons' are equipped with a hose-drum unit in the weapons bay to allow them to refuel other Soviet reconnaissance aircraft.

chief task of the Soviet aircraft, but 'ferret' flights are also regularly undertaken. Interceptions are frequently carried out by Western fighters around the coasts of Europe, North America and Japan, where the Soviet snoopers test air defences for weaknesses in much the same way as Western aircraft have been doing for years around the Soviet Union. Flights are mounted from a number of bases. 'Bears' from airfields on the Kola peninsula around Murmansk fly missions into the North Sea and North Atlantic, and either return to their home base or continue down the eastern seaboard of the United States before landing on Cuba. In the Far East Soviet aircraft regularly patrol the Alaskan coast from bases on the Kamchatka peninsula, while aircraft based around Vladivostok probe Japanese airspace before heading

south to the ex-American air base at Cam Ranh Bay in Vietnam, where a squadron of Tu-16 'Badgers' is also based. During the 1970s many Soviet long-range aircraft flew from Egyptian bases, often wearing spurius Egyptian markings.

High-speed 'Blinder'

A limited high-speed high-altitude maritime reconnaissance capability has been provided by the Tupolev Tu-22 'Blinder-C' aircraft, which not only carries a battery of cameras in its bomb bay, but also many Elint antennae. These aircraft are often intercepted over the Baltic Sea. The 1970s saw the advent of specialist Sigint aircraft flying for the Soviet forces. The ancient Ilyushin Il-14 'Crate' was widely used, but the prime aircraft was the Antonov An-12 'Cub-B', a conversion of the Hercules-type 'Cub' transport in widespread use with Soviet forces. Seen in many configurations, the 'Cub-B's' capacious cabin allows the carriage of many sensors for eavesdropping. Some aircraft have been seen wearing Egyptian or even Aeroflot colours. Indeed, regular airliners of the Soviet state airline have often been accused of spying during scheduled flights to Western coun-

Above: Released in 1987, this remarkable photograph shows the Soviet base at Cam Ranh Bay in Vietnam, from where reconnaissance aircraft have operated for many years. A squadron of 'Badgers' is lined up, with five 'Bears'. The camera platform is probably an SR-71.

Right: Several 'Badger' electronic reconnaissance versions exist, including the 'Badger-D'. The variant is identified by nose radar and underfuselage bulges. Like other Soviet reconnaissance aircraft, these are regularly seen around US Navy battle groups, and are often escorted by Tomcat fighters.

tries, deviating from their flight paths to overfly military establishments. Since the cessation of Egyptian operations, Soviet snoopers have been able to operate from bases in Libya and South Yemen. One further important type introduced during the 1970s was the Ilyushin Il-20 'Coot-A' conversion of the trusty Il-18 airliner, this sprouting an inordinate number of antennae and fairings. A giant canoe fairing under the forward fuselage is believed to house a SLAR, for creating radar imagery similar to that gleaned by the Boeing RC-135s.

Photo 'Foxbat'

While the Soviet Union's Sigint gathering effort built up dramatically during the 1960s and 1970s, to rival and perhaps surpass that of the West, the Photint mission had been largely untouched (apart from the abortive Yak-25RD) until the appearance in 1971 of a reconnaissance version of the excellent MiG-25 'Foxbat' fighter. Designated MiG-25R, this aircraft made its debut in Egypt where four were deployed to aid Egyptian forces in assessing Israeli military advances. During early flights the MiG-25R 'Foxbat-B' was clocked at speeds up to Mach 3.2 and at altitudes over 70,000 ft (21330 m). No Israeli fighter could approach that performance, and the MiG-25Rs embarked on a series of overflights to photograph Israeli installations. Due to political difficulties the 'Foxbats' returned to the Soviet Union during

1972. Later, in 1973, they returned briefly.

During these flights it was obvious to the West that the Soviets now possessed an aircraft which, although not quite matching the performance of the SR-71, could operate with impunity over areas with anything less than state-of-the-art defences. The 'Foxbat-B' carried a small SLAR and five cameras in its nose, and could produce excellent imagery during overflights. Following Israel, Iran was

Below: Much of the Soviet Sigint effort is aimed at naval forces, aircraft such as this 'Badger-F' being used to catalogue radar fits of NATO ships. This aircraft veers away from its RAF pursuer low over the North Sea.

Antonov An-12 'Cub-B'

For many years the standard Soviet transport, the Antonov An-12 was an obvious choice for carrying large amounts of Sigint equipment owing to its voluminous cabin and healthy range. 'Cub-B' is the Sigint version, seen in many forms over the years, in the past wearing Aeroflot or Egyptian air force markings. Other 'Cub' variants are used for countermeasures and equipment trials work, although their behaviour indicates a secondary reconnaissance role.

next to receive the attentions of the MiG-25R, which carried out a series of overflights until delivery to the Shah's air force of the Grumman F-14 Tomcat, together with its Phoenix missiles, halted further forays. Since that time the MiG-25R has been active over Afghanistan, watching developments in neighbouring Pakistan and around the borders of China. 'Foxbat-Bs' have been exported to Algeria, Iraq, Libya, India and Syria, and those of Syria and Iraq have been active against Israel and Iran respectively,

Left: This civilian registered aircraft is a 'Cub-B' Sigint platform, its identity given away by the radomes under the forward fuselage. Based on the An-12 transport, the 'Cub-B' can carry bulky equipment and many operators in its cabin.

Below: Do not believe the smart colour scheme and Aeroflot titles of this An-12, for it is a 'Cub-B' and its purpose could not be further from airline use. Small aerials under the fuselage and under the wings serve a comprehensive Sigint suite inside. 'Cub-Bs' have been seen in several configurations.

Mikoyan-Gurevich MiG-25R 'Foxbat-D'

Only the Lockheed SR-71 surpasses the MiG-25 for altitude and speed performance. The two reconnaissance versions are the fastest of the breed, differentiated by a slimmer nose profile and straight wings (those of the fighter are slightly kinked). Nearly 200 are operational with Soviet forces, mostly comprising 'Foxbat-Bs' with a small SLAR and cameras. The remainder are 'Foxbat-Ds', which uplift a large SLAR and Sigint equipment. Libya has also been supplied with a small number of both variants, while Algeria, Syria, Iraq and India operate 'Foxbat-Bs'. In foreign service these high-performance spies are often flown by Soviet personnel.

although probably under tight Soviet control.

An altogether more strategic version of the MiG-25R emerged during the mid-1970s, this being the 'Foxbat-D'. Large dielectric panels on each side of the nose hide a much larger SLAR than carried by the 'Foxbat-B', and other antennae serve a Sigint suite. The oblique-looking SLARs are used during peripheral flights, such as those undertaken along the East-West German border, the radar peering into West Germany to record military installations. Such operations have occasionally involved unintentional overflights of West German territory, largely caused by the lack of manoeuvrability of the 'Foxbat' when operating at high speed and altitude. No doubt the Lockheed SR-71 has similarly violated WarPac airspace during its reconnaissance runs down the western side of the border.

US high-fliers

The 'Foxbat's' high-flying Western counterparts, the Lockheed SR-71A and U-2R, continued their successful careers throughout the 1970s, being heavily involved in the Middle East air war. Completely redesigned

Whereas the SR-71 featured intricate engineering and brilliant aerodynamic design, the MiG-25 relies on brute strength for its performance. Fastest variants are the reconnaissance MiG-25Rs, exemplified here by a 'Foxbat-B' with a battery of cameras in the nose. The dark panel on the side of the nose hides a SLAR.

Spyplane

from its illustrious forebears, the U-2R introduced long endurance and good sensor payload, qualities first enjoyed over China and Vietnam. It became a regular operator from the RAF base at Akrotiri on Cyprus, from where aircraft could monitor events in the Middle East, such as the truce following the 1973 Yom Kippur war, as well as the continuing Soviet ICBM development in the southern USSR. Aircraft operating from Akrotiri were often seen carrying vast 'farms' of antennae on the lower rear fuselage, while SLARs peered through flat panels in the large 'superpods' carried under the wings. Similar sensor fits were often seen in Europe, where aircraft became regular visitors to RAF Mildenhall in England during the latter half of the decade. The days of the older U-2 versions were not entirely numbered, for U-2Cs appeared in England at RAF Wethersfield and RAF Upper Heyford, from where they carried out equipment tests for a radar location system. These aircraft carried a two-tone grey paint scheme that had been adopted to dispel the suspicion aroused in England by all-black U-2s. Operating under the *Pave Onyx/Pave Nickel* programmes, the U-2Cs were involved in many missions in Europe,

The slender body and huge wings of the Lockheed U-2R were much in evidence wherever US reconnaissance units gathered. A major upgrade involved the fitment of 'superpods' to the wings, enabling them to carry even more sensors.

and indeed lost an aircraft in a highly-publicized crash in West Germany.

Lockheed SR-71s continued their work around the borders of the Soviet Union, while stepping up operations against North Korea. It is alleged that North Korea has fired several SA-2 missiles at the 'Blackbird', but none have scored. Indeed, tantalizing rumours have surfaced from many areas of the globe, including Israel, that attempts have been made to down the SR-71, but its phenomenal performance has kept it out of trouble. Cuba was a regular stamping ground for the SR-71, with a brief moratorium on overflights between 1977 and 1979. Advances in military capability (particularly in the field of Soviet aid) have been monitored in such a way, aided by peripheral missions flown by U-2Rs. Europe became a major area for SR-71 operations in 1976, with the beginning of short deployments to RAF Mildenhall for missions over the Baltic, German border and North Cape regions.

Navy advances

Development in the United States' Sigint gathering field has been upheld too, with the introduction of new types and new variants.

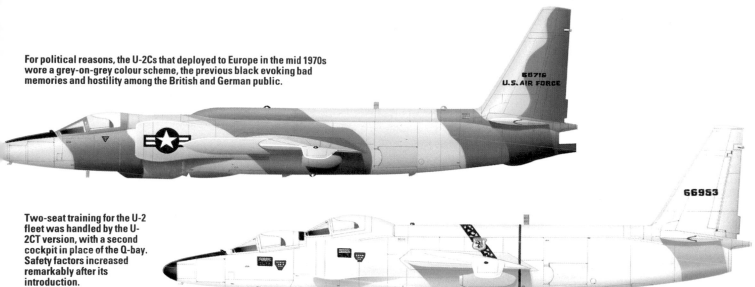

For political reasons, the U-2Cs that deployed to Europe in the mid 1970s wore a grey-on-grey colour scheme, the previous black evoking bad memories and hostility among the British and German public.

Two-seat training for the U-2 fleet was handled by the U-2CT version, with a second cockpit in place of the Q-bay. Safety factors increased remarkably after its introduction.

Far right: This U-2C crashed in West Germany during May 1975. Here USAF crew undertake the recovery of the wreckage.

Below: A U-2C is caught on finals to RAF Wethersfield, from where many of the 'Pave Onyx'/'Pave Nickel' trials took place. Noticeable on the wings are the 'slipper' fuel tanks and a radar warning receiver.

The US Navy began operations in 1971 with the Lockheed EP-3E version of the Orion. For two years previous it had operated the EP-3B, but with the E-model it introduced great capability for its primary role of naval Sigint. Replacing the EC-121 Constellations, the EP-3Es went to work with VQ-1 and VQ-2, which were still operating the Douglas EA-3B Skywarrior. Inheriting some of the equipment from their predecessors, such as the *Big Look* SAM warning system and the *Deepwell* communications intercept system, the EP-3E also introduced equipment for the classification of Soviet naval radars. Identified by a large

Spyplane

At the beginning of the 1980s, the 9th SRW's SR-71 fleet began receiving an altogether more sinister colour scheme of flat-black all over, with only red stencilling to break the appearance. This black paint contains iron balls to absorb radar energy.

Three of VQ-1's Lockheed EP-3E Orions pose for the camera. Careful scrutinisation reveals three differing antenna fits, a feature of several Sigint aircraft fleets.

dorsal canoe fairing and others under the fuselage, it has recently adopted equipment for the task of Rint. This involves measuring the radiation unintentionally emitted by radars and other installations while in a stand-by mode. Such techniques are useful for detection and identification of vessels, even if sailing under full communications and radar silence.

RC-135 update

These Rint techniques were also introduced to the US Air Force's fleet of Boeing RC-135s, which underwent a series of radical modifications and updates throughout the 1970s and early 1980s. The 6th SW at Eielson in Alaska received the first of its RC-135S aircraft in 1969, and has used the type for reconnaissance purposes ever since. Primarily concerned with Telint gathering, the RC-135S aircraft had large circular windows through which cameras could photograph Soviet re-entry vehicles during ICBM tests targeted to the Sea of Okhotsk. To reduce glare during re-entry photography the starboard wing and engine nacelles of RC-135S aircraft were painted black. Appearing in many configurations, including varying

Douglas EA-3B Skywarrior

Lovingly referred to as the 'Whale', the electronic reconnaissance variant of the Skywarrior has graced US carrier decks since 1958. A few early EA-3As preceded the definitive EA-3B into service with VQ-1 and VQ-2, the Pacific and Atlantic Fleet Reconnaissance Squadrons. Equipment carried is largely for Elint, and roughly equates to that carried by the EP-3E Orion, although less sophisticated due to the limitations of airframe size. A flight crew of three is backed up by four equipment operators seated internally.

numbers of windows, 'towel rail' antennae, blister and teardrop fairings on the rear fuselage, the RC-135S aircraft appear to be modified regularly to meet new Soviet missile advances. One constant feature is the 'thimble' nose.

The main body of US Air Force Sigint gatherers also underwent a modernization programme, initiated by the conversion of

Below: The first RC-135S seen shortly after its conversion from RC-135D standard. The 'towel rail' antennae intercepted Soviet missile guidance data during Telint flights from Alaskan and Aleutian bases. This aircraft crashed in 1969.

Right: Carrierborne Elint gathering capability is provided by the Douglas EA-3B, dubbed the 'Whale' due to its size. This size is graphically demonstrated here, as 'Nimitz' crewmen flex muscles while manhandling this VQ-1 Skywarrior.

Boeing RC-135V

14844

Conversion of the 55th SRW's RC-135C fleet to RC-135V standard occurred during the early 1970s, resulting in a fleet of eight aircraft, joined later by the six RC-135Ws. Forming the basis of the US Sigint fleet, these aircraft carry extensive recording, analysis, direction-finding and track-breaking equipment to gather Sigint of any nature. The cheek SLARs generate radar imagery of high quality from long oblique ranges. Crew size varies from mission to mission and from variant to variant, but usually involves around 17 operators in addition to the four flight crew.

Above: Following their Southeast Asia service, the RC-135Ms of the 82nd SRS at Kadena received a smart paint scheme and continued their Far East operations.

Below: This fine study of an RC-135V on approach displays the huge blade aerials under the fuselage. Note the five non-standard mission marks on the nose.

three of the 55th SRW's RC-135Cs to RC-135U standard. As recounted earlier this added large amounts of new and highly sophisticated equipment, for the RC-135Us were used for deployments around the globe, often on special missions. The seven remaining RC-135Cs began converting to RC-135V standard in 1973, this new configuration adding the 'thimble' nose and huge blade aerials beneath the centre section on which were secured oval-shaped plates. At the same time other smaller antennae were installed, together with an updating of some onboard systems. The first RC-135U followed suit in 1977 to form the basic Sigint fleet. Now serving with the 55th SRW, the six RC-135Ms which had bravely struggled through the war in South East Asia were refitted during the early 1980s to RC-135W standard, similar to the RC-135V but with minor differences and improvements. Apart from the major refits, the RC-135 story has been one of constant

39792

Above: During the early 1980s the six RC-135Ms were upgraded to RC-135W standard, roughly similar to the RC-135V. Now serving with the 55th SRW, the RC-135Ws fly alongside the Vs on global reconnaissance tasks. Here one of them refuels over the Pacific from a KC-135A.

Below: Two of the RC-135Us remain on the strength of the 55th SRW, employed in many parts of the world on various missions. The badge on the nose of this aircraft is that bestowed on Soviet units that have achieved excellence, a playful joke for the RC crews aimed at their Soviet shadowers.

Above: An RC-135W taxis out of the East Anglian mist for an early morning departure from RAF Mildenhall. RC-135s continue the USAF tradition of using English bases.

small changes to meet the ever-shifting electronic environment, and constant evaluation of new forms of sensors.

Such developments have been a feature of another new type brought on to the scene during the 1970s, the British Aerospace Nimrod. No. 51 Squadron's Comets had served valiantly since 1958, but a replacement was sorely needed. First delivered to the RAF in 1971, three special variants of the Nimrod maritime patroller arrived at Wyton to fill the requirement. Owing to the immense amount of special equipment that had to be fitted on board, it was not to be until May 1974 that the Nimrod R.Mk 1 could take up operations and allow the venerable Comets to retire gracefully. With excellent range and an increase in power and internal volume, the Nimrods were a welcome change for No. 51's crews. Canberra B.Mk 6s continued in use for a

Left: The role of electronic surveillance has never been admitted by the UK Ministry of Defence, but if proof of the task undertaken by the Nimrod R.Mk 1 is needed, then this photograph taken by the Swedish air force over the Baltic should suffice.

Below: No 51 Sqn's Canberra fleet remained active until 1976, with four B.Mk 6 (mod) aircraft. This example is in typical 1970s configuration, with 'whips', 'warts' and a tactical two-tone camouflage.

Above: At the end of its career, this Canberra B.Mk 6 (mod) retired to the secret base at Akrotiri, from where it had flown many missions in the Middle East and southern WarPac areas.

Below: This modified Vickers Varsity was on the strength of No 51 Sqn although it wears a calibration colour scheme. It probably operated Sigint missions along the Berlin corridor.

Above: Bringing with it a welcome increase of internal volume, performance and range, No 51 Sqn had to wait three years after delivery before the British Aerospace Nimrod R.Mk 1 could begin operations.

Below: Early Nimrod R.Mk 1s differed little from their maritime patrol cousins, identified by the short radome in place of the MAD sting in the tail. They have been progressively updated with more equipment.

British Aerospace Nimrod R.Mk 1

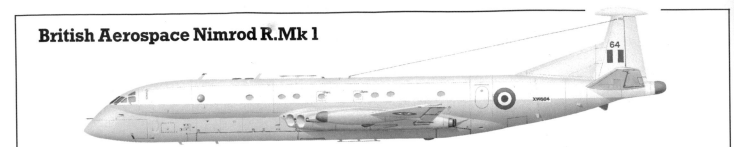

The introduction into service of the Nimrod MR.Mk 1 maritime patroller gave the RAF the airframe it needed to replace the ageing Comets. Delivered in 1971, the three Nimrod R.Mk 1s underwent three years of being fitted with specialised equipment for their reconnaissance task. Serving with No 51 Sqn, the trio replaced the Comet on the advanced Sigint task, and were soon encountered over the Baltic by Swedish, and no doubt Soviet, fighters. No details have ever been released concerning the size of the crew, but it is safe to assume a large number of equipment operators.

Above: This solitary Hawker Siddeley Andover C.Mk 1 (mod) served No 51 Sqn on Sigint tasks for some years, appearing at various bases in the Mediterranean. It later served with the Electronic Warfare Avionics Unit.

Above right: Still wearing its No 46 Sqn badge, the Andover C.Mk 1 (mod) sprouts several antennae to cast suspicion on its supposed transport role. It was, of course, serving with No 51 at the time.

Below: This was the last Sigint Canberra used by No 51, seen in 1976. With its warty excrescence, it was designated B.Mk 6BS.

B.Mk 2MRRs of No. 27 Sqn. For the RAF's Photint role the Canberra PR.Mk 9 remained the main platform.

European activities

further two years after the Nimrod's introduction, these last few aircraft being noted with some extremely bizarre sensor fits, including 'thimble' noses and large wart-like turrets projecting from immediately behind the cockpit. Withdrawn in 1976, the Canberras left the Nimrods as the RAF's only Sigint asset, although a sole Hawker Siddeley Andover C.Mk 1(mod), nominally on the strength of the RAF's Electronic Warfare Avionics Unit (an equipment test unit), was occasionally seen around Europe during the late 1970s wearing No. 51's badge, fuelling rumours that it too was involved in operational evaluations of some Sigint equipment. Also withdrawn in 1974 were the Victor SR.Mk 2s of No. 543 Sqn, whose tasks were by now almost completely maritime; this role was picked up by the Avro Vulcan

For long the domain of the United States, United Kingdom and Soviet Union, the role of strategic reconnaissance spread rapidly to other nations during the 1970s. Sweden had operated specially-equipped Canberra and Vickers Viking aircraft for some years on eavesdropping missions, but their place was taken in 1971 by the far larger and more sophisticated Aérospatiale Caravelle. With the local designation Tp-85 and differing from the airliner version by having a plethora of aerials and fairings, including an extended nosecone and a canoe fairing under the forward fuselage, the two Caravelles have flown under the banner of the Forsokcentralen on electronic listening missions around the Warsaw Pact nations. Other aircraft employed by Sweden include the maritime reconnaissance version of the Saab Viggen fighter, which has been used for snooping around Soviet ships sailing in the Baltic. In-

Above: The short tail radome housing a conical helix receiver is demonstrated by this Nimrod R.Mk 1. Three such aircraft were delivered, all based at RAF Wyton.

Above: For the first four years of the decade, the Handley Page Victor SR.Mk 2 continued in the strategic reconnaissance role. As the years went by, this tasking turned away from the Soviet Union and more towards high-altitude maritime surveillance.

Right: In 1974 the Victor SR.Mk 2 was replaced by the Avro Vulcan B.Mk 2 MRR, which flew with No 27 Sqn from Scampton. Serving until 1982, the Vulcan's introduction completed the V-bomber trio that had performed the strategic and maritime reconnaissance task.

deed, the fighter version of the Viggen has seen perhaps more intercepts of strategic reconnaissance aircraft than any other type, as spying aircraft from both East and West regularly infringe Swedish airspace during operations over the Baltic.

French operations

France had toyed with reconnaissance aircraft earlier (with the alleged use of Air France airliners), but it was not until the arrival in service in 1977 of a specially-modified version of the well-known Douglas DC-8 airliner that a dedicated Sigint type was

Below: High-altitude Photint and infra-red reconnaissance requirements for the RAF remained the task of the Canberra PR.Mk 9.

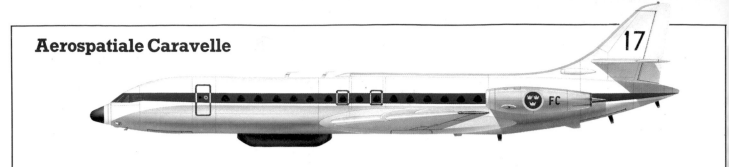

Aerospatiale Caravelle

Sweden has long maintained a Sigint effort of its own, aimed at Warsaw Pact forces which threaten the neutrality of this Scandinavian country. Replacing Canberras and Vikings in the task of strategic electronic reconnaissance are two ex-airliner Caravelles, suitably modified with canoe fairings, blade aerials and 'thimble' nose, and designated Tp-85. Performing most of their task in the Baltic, the two aircraft originally flew with the Forsokcentralen (note the 'FC' code), but now carry the marks of F13 wing, flying from Malmslatt.

Another nation to operate Sigint Canberras was Sweden, which flew this example over the Baltic.

France's strategic reconnaissance requirements are met by the Dassault Mirage IVA, which carries a CT-52 reconnaissance pod under the fuselage.

included in the inventory. Chief features of this single aircraft are wingtip SLAR pods. French Photint requirements rely on the Dassault-Breguet Mirage IVA, a version of the Mach 2 bomber with a bomb bay pallet packed with cameras and some electronic sensors. The third type of Frence reconnaissance aircraft employed on strategic tasks is the elderly Nord Noratlas which, equipped with electronic receivers, has appeared over the Baltic.

West Germany also joined the ranks of the spying nations when it received five Dassault-Breguet Atlantics which had been fitted out by the American E-Systems company with delicate listening gear. Constantly updated and sprouting ever more antennae, the Atlantics have been a regular fixture over the Baltic Sea, where their sophisticated electronic sensors have been tuned to WarPac military advances, both on and off the water. Four of these converted maritime patrol aircraft were returned for a major update in 1980, while their undeclared war against Communist radars and communications continued unabated. Tactical reconnaissance missions flown by German navy Lockheed RF-104 Starfighters also furnished much information of a strategic nature.

Low-level spying

In a similar fashion, Poland and Czechoslovakia employed Mikoyan-Gurevich MiG-21RF aircraft for low-level reconnaissance flights along German and Danish coasts,

French EW and Elint work has been carried out by a handful of Nord Noratlases. This ageing transport has a large cabin to take the equipment and operators. Serving with Escadre Electronique 54, they often operate over the Baltic.

Above: Three Canberra B.Mk 2s were supplied to West Germany in 1966 for target-towing duties, but they were fitted out with special survey equipment instead. Allegations suggest that they were used on espionage flights – they have certainly been regular visitors to British bases.

these aircraft carrying their sensors in an underfuselage pod. Poland also introduced a limited Sigint capability with the elderly Ilyushin Il-14 airliner and equally old Il-28 bomber. In the Middle East, Israel also highlighted the dramatic escalation of Sigint operators around the world, at first using converted Boeing KC-97s and then Boeing 707 airliners for clandestine surveillance of its Arab neighbours.

Central America

During 1981 strategic reconnaissance aircraft embarked on a new campaign, this time against Nicaragua. For some time the military build-up in that country had been the focus of the high-resolution cameras of overflying U-2Rs, and a presentation to the press of some of the results followed in March 1982. In the ensuing months Nicaragua

claimed that its airspace had been violated many times since 1981 by US Air Force spyplanes, the majority of them RC-135s, with further penetrations by U-2Rs and SR-71s. Such flights have been undertaken to monitor military advances, while another type of mission was being mounted to ascertain whether the Communist Nicaraguan government was supplying arms to guerrillas in neighbouring El Salvador. Using unarmed Lockheed AC-130 Hercules, these missions have been flown at night to try and spot infiltrators. The AC-130 is best remembered as the truck-killing gunship of the Vietnam War, and its sophisticated night detection gear rendered it perfect for the reconnaissance task required over El Salvador. Forward-looking infra-red, low-light-level TV, Starlite night vision scopes, moving target radars and 'Black Crow' truck ignition detec-

West Germany has joined the Sigint game with the Dassault-Breguet Atlantic. Five Sigint-configured aircraft were delivered under the 'Peace Peek' programme, serving with MFG 3 at Nordholz alongside regular patrol Atlantics.

Although primarily a tactical reconnaissance type, the MiG-21RF 'Fishbed-H' makes many reconnaissance runs along the North German coast for the Polish air force. The underfuselage pod contains cameras and infra-red sensors.

Left: The Soviet Union and other WarPac nations such as Poland operate an Elint version of the Ilyushin Il-14 'Crate'. Several are seen around West German and Danish waters.

Above: The sophisticated onboard sensors of the Lockheed AC-130, normally used for locating targets for the fearsome guns, have obvious uses for reconnaissance missions. Such flights have been undertaken in Central America.

comment on rumours that the AC-130s have been as active over Nicaragua itself as over the Salvadorean border.

Not to be outdone, the US Army has been highly active in the spying game in Central America. Successes during the South East Asia conflict of the small battlefield Sigint aircraft have led this to become a major role in US Army Aviation, with Beech RU-21s and new RC-12s based and active in several

Below: Grumman's OV-1D Mohawk has also been used in Central America, alongside other US Army snoopers such as the Beech RU-21.

tors gave any arms smugglers on the ground little chance of escaping detection. Results from these missions have not been forthcoming, and the Pentagon is equally loathe to

Above: The huge radar carried above the Boeing E-3 Sentry's back and the extensive onboard communications suite have allowed the type to make contributions to the reconnaissance effort in Central America. E-3s regularly patrol the area to spot any aerial movement.

Right: What the US spyplanes are looking for in Central America are scenes such as this, depicting a Nicaraguan airfield under construction. Obviously such an airfield could pose major problems to US interests, so a keen eye is kept on all military developments on the ground.

parts of the world. Among those is Honduras, where RU-21s are believed to have carried out Comint missions along that country's border with Nicaragua. Also stationed in Honduras have been the Grumman OV-1 Mohawks of the US Army, whose radar and infra-red sensors are particularly useful in detecting Nicaraguan units moving under the dense jungle. Finally, the Boeing E-3 Sentry airborne early warning aircraft has also been used over Central America for reconnaissance purposes, its powerful radar detecting

small aircraft trying to smuggle arms to Communist guerrillas in El Salvador.

Another war in the early 1980s involved strategic reconnaissance aircraft as they aided the overt forces to fight the battle. It was an Argentine Elint Lockheed Neptune which first detected the British Task Force sailing south to recapture the Falkland Islands,

Much of the Photint generated over Nicaragua has come from the Lockheed U-2 and SR-71. This is a U-2R, a type which has accounted for many violations of Nicaraguan airspace, which cannot at present be defended by high-altitude SAMs.

Spyplane

Argentina's rag bag air forces contained this Lockheed Neptune, configured for providing the navy with Sigint. It was this type which first alerted the High Command of the approaching British Task Force sailing to relieve the islands.

Little is known of No 51 Sqn's role in the battle for the Falklands, except that they operated from Ascension during the conflict. Other operations may have taken place from Chile. This single aircraft received an inflight-refuelling probe for South Atlantic missions.

RAF Canberra PR.Mk 9s may have made overflights of Argentina from Chilean bases and wearing Chilean markings. This aircraft is one of the three that were delivered legitimately to Chile shortly after the war.

while hastily-converted Handley Page Victors revived their radar reconnaissance role to provide much-needed intelligence on Argentine shipping and military dispositions prior to the Task Force's arrival in the war zone. These missions were somewhat ironic, for the Victor had been replaced in this role by the Avro Vulcan back in 1974, yet the Vulcan reconnaissance squadron had been disbanded two days before the Argentinians invaded the islands! Equipment was crammed back into four Victor tankers, and their crews underwent a rapid training course. The reconnaissance missions proved highly successful and several were made before probe-equipped Nimrod maritime patrol

aircraft could take up the task.

Very little information surrounds operations from Chile during the Falklands war, yet certain evidence points to the fact that up to six RAF Canberra PR.Mk 9s may have operated from the Chilean base at Punta Arenas in Chilean air force markings. Obviously the use of the high-flying Canberras over and around Argentina would have been of enormous use to the United Kingdom, with both optical and infra-red sensors available to monitor Argentine air activity in particular, yet confirmation of this operation does not exist. What is known is that three further Canberra PR.Mk 9 aircraft were delivered to Chile after the Argentine surrender, perhaps as a 'thank-you' for services rendered during the war. Even less information surrounds the contribution made by No. 51 Sqn to the Falklands war effort. Indeed, the only knowledge concerns the bestowal of a South Atlantic Battle Honour upon the RAF's premier Sigint squadron, and the fact that one of its Nimrod R.Mk 1s was fitted with an inflight-refuelling probe to allow operations in the war zone from the main operating base on Ascension Island. Rumours suggest that No. 51 operated from Chile too, but with a virtual black-out of knowledge such rumours remain pure speculation. What is certain is that the potential importance to the British command of No. 51's peculiar talents when

directed towards Argentina needs no supposition.

KAL 007

Over a year after the British had regained the Falklands, in September 1983 the world was shaken by the news that a Korean Air Lines Boeing 747 had been downed near the island of Sakhalin in the Soviet Far East, with 269 people on board. The ensuing furore established that the Soviets had allegedly mistaken the tragic airliner for a Boeing RC-135S aircraft operating from Alaska. Indeed, such an aircraft was flying that night, and had even crossed the path of the doomed airliner, but had landed at its base an hour before the 747 was shot down. The airliner had penetrated Soviet airspace twice during its fatal flight, once over the Kamchatka peninsula and then over Sakhalin. For over an hour it had been shadowed by MiG-23 'Flogger' and Sukhoi Su-21 'Flagon' fighters, none of whose pilots had apparently reported it as a civil airliner; all believed it was another RC-135 involved in a spy flight in conjunction with a Soviet missile test under way at the time. However, the Soviet pilots have been intercepting RC-135s in this piece of the world for years, and their radar operators are well-versed in the racetrack patterns traced by the Telint gatherers from Alaska. The Soviet Union has stuck rigidly to its story that, civil airliner or not, the aircraft was involved in a premeditated spy flight. The truth will probably never be known outside of privileged circles, but the incident highlighted the dangers of strategic reconnaissance, where the slightest misinterpretation of intentions could have disastrous consequences. The spotlight was also shone briefly on the otherwise secretive RC-135, and its Comint capabilities were illustrated by the release of transcripts of radio talk between Soviet fighters.

Top: After the Korean Air Lines shootdown, there was much activity in the area. This Soviet Ilyushin Il-14 Elint aircraft is escorted through the shootdown zone by US Navy aircraft.

Above: A Sukhoi Su-21 'Flagon' such as this one fired the fatal missiles at the Korean Boeing 747. A transcript of fighter communications recorded by an RC-135 was published in the political aftermath.

Below: Soviet fighter pilots apparently confused the 747 with this aircraft, an RC-135S of the 6th SW, which was flying a Telint mission on the fateful night. The Soviets allege that they mistook the airliner for another RC-135.

Contemporary Situations

Left: Training for the 9th SRW SR-71 crews is handled on the single SR-71B, with a second raised cockpit and additional ventral fins. The SR-71 still represents the most capable reconnaissance aircraft, able to carry Photint, IR or Sigint sensors at great speed and altitude.

Leading the Sigint field are the USAF's Boeing RC-135s, which have become increasingly involved in Rint disciplines. This is a 55th SRW RC-135W, departing a wet and windy Mildenhall runway.

Today the strategic reconnaissance aircraft is a fixed part of the world's military aviation scene; no more is it the expensive plaything of the superpowers. More and more nations receive aircraft capable of the electronic surveillance mission, even if it is a low-cost utility type with rudimentary gear on board. At the other end of the spectrum the superpowers push forward the science and technology of the art at alarming pace.

Recent years have seen a massive increase in the importance of strategic reconnaissance aircraft to the world's air forces. Advances in electronics have allowed more and more nations to possess Sigint aircraft, and the role is becoming a regular part of a nation's defences. For long the domain of the two superpowers and a handful of other nations, the electronic eavesdropping mission is now affordable for any nation that desires the capability.

Prime mover in terms of technology is the United States, which operates a number of aircraft types on the strategic mission, with no expense spared. Sigint gathering is primarily handled by the Boeing RC-135 fleet,

which goes from strength to strength in terms of snooping capability. The fleet is split between the 6th SW and the 55th SRW. The former is primarily concerned with Telint, operating from its Alaskan base at Eielson, and from the forward-operating base of Shemya, at the Soviet end of the Aleutian island chain. Two RC-135S and one RC-135X aircraft are on charge, together with the TC-135S Telint trainer. The remainder of the RC-135 fleet consists of two U-models, eight V-models and six W-models, all of which serve with the 55th SRW from its base at Offutt. These continue the task for which they have been used since the mid-1960s, namely global electronic reconnaissance.

Spyplane

An RC-135V receives pre-mission maintenance at Mildenhall. Just visible is the open cargo door, which allows quick and easy changes of onboard equipment. Pre-flight checks obviously involve the removal of many red tags!

SR-71 carries a wide variety of sensors, from optical cameras to SLARs. Sigint equipment is often allied to imaging sensors to give an overall sight, sound and electronic picture of the situation, a feat which is performed excellently by the SR-71, its cameras or radar beams peering far into the target nation from its high-altitude perch. The US Air Force is reticent when discussing the true performance of the SR-71, but it seems likely that the speed is around Mach 3.5 and ceiling nearly 100,000 ft (30480 m). Approaching 25 years of service, the SR-71 has still much to offer the intelligence community and there is no sign of a cutback in operations.

'Dragon Lady'

Also soldiering on is the Lockheed U-2R, serving alongside the SR-71 with the 9th SRW. As well as mounting missions from Beale, the U-2s fly regularly from Florida over the Caribbean; from Akrotiri on Cyprus for Mediterranean, Middle East and southern

Equipped with a bewildering array of sensors for Elint, Comint, Rint and radar imagery, the RC-135s are also believed to carry jamming equipment to allow them to 'stir up' Soviet defences. Deploying regularly from Offutt, the 55th SRW fleet operates from a number of bases around the world. From Mildenhall in England the snoopers patrol the western edges of the Soviet Union, particularly over the Baltic Sea and around the North Cape. From Hellenikon in Greece the 55th SRW can monitor the southern USSR, the Middle East and the Mediterranean. Libya has been a particular target for the RC-135's attentions in recent years. On Okinawa, RC-135s are based at Kadena for flights in the Far East aimed at North Korea, Vietnam and the Soviet Union, while in the Americas RC-135s fly regular missions over the Caribbean and Central America from bases in Florida.

'Blackbirds' in Europe

Operating over the same areas as the RC-135s, the Lockheed SR-71s of the 9th SRW are active from Mildenhall and Kadena in addition to their home base of Beale in California. At each of the three operating locations are situated support fleets of Boeing KC-135Q tankers, which carry the special JP-7 fuel needed by the 'Blackbird'. Today the

Approaching the tanker is an RC-135W. Inflight-refuelling allows the RC-135 to stay on station for well over 24 hours, aircraft often carrying relief crews for these marathon flights. An area at the rear of the aircraft contains bunks to allow off-duty personnel to rest before their next period on-watch.

Below: The pair of RC-135Us feature a considerably different antenna fit from their cousins, and are thought to undertake much experimental work.

Right: Based in Alaska, the 6th SW's pair of RC-135S aircraft are employed on Telint duties, their configuration constantly altering to match Soviet missile advances.

Above: Lockheed TR-1s have picked up many of the strategic missions performed by the U-2R. Ice forms on the wing during the long descent from altitude.

Soviet flights; and from Osan AB in South Korea to monitor military advances in the North. European operations are handled by a new version of the 'Dragon Lady', the Lockheed TR-1A. This new aircraft is virtually identical to the U-2R, but features updated secondary systems and is primarily aimed at a new role, namely that of tactical reconnaissance. Based at Alconbury in England with the 17th Reconnaissance Wing, the TR-

Left: SR-71, U-2 and TR-1 pilots wear the S-1010B pressure suit to protect them in the event of depressurisation at altitude. To avoid nitrogen poisoning they pre-breathe oxygen for an hour before take off.

Below: One can almost feel the immense power of the SR-71 as it burns off into typical English weather from Mildenhall. A full-time detachment is maintained here.

Above: An SR-71 turns on to Mildenhall's runway prior to departure. Missions from this base are aimed primarily at the Soviet Union's western side, such as the Baltic or North Cape, but other areas such as the Middle East and Libya are sometimes covered from here.

Below: Bad weather makes the SR-71 even more sinister, its remarkable shape unique amongst aircraft. Recent additions include radar warning receivers in the forward chines, which interrupt the smooth lines. These serve a complex onboard electronic countermeasures suite.

Housed in the Boeing E-3's rotodome is a radar scanner and IFF interrogator, used primarily for airborne early warning purposes. Nevertheless, surveillance by E-3s can generate intelligence of a useful nature to strategic planning, as has been demonstrated over Central America.

Airborne command posts such as this Boeing EC-135H can on occasion be particularly useful for Comint collection. It is alleged that these Mildenhall-based aircraft flew such missions in the wake of the Chernobyl nuclear disaster.

1s are tasked with providing high-altitude stand-off reconnaissance of the European battlefield. Utilising side-looking synthetic aperture radars as their chief sensor, the TR-1 can peer far across the border, spotting tank formations and other military installations at long distance, thus giving ground commanders far greater knowledge of the rear echelons and infrastructure of any potential War-Pac attack. Of course, such capability can be equally useful to government agencies during peacetime, and it is no mistake that the TR-1 can carry all of the sensors used by the U-2R. TR-1s have been seen with large antenna farms similar to those carried by U-2Rs

operating from Mildenhall during the late 1970s and early 1980s. Such sensor fits have been accompanied by specially modified superpods which appear to contain airborne radars. Despite the 'tactical reconnaissance' tag applied by the US Air Force, and the openness with which the service talks about the TR-1, the aircraft is certainly involved on missions similar to those of its altogether more secret U-2R predecessor.

USAF miscellany

Various other aircraft are operated on clandestine missions by the US Air Force. Often used as a basis for covert reconnaissance, the

Lockheed Hercules still performs such tasks today with at least two distinct versions in use. The first is the EC-130E, characterized by a huge dorsal fin fillet and equally outsize blade aerials under the outer wing panels. Noted in two configurations, little is known about these aircraft operated by the 193rd Electronic Combat Squadron, Pennsylvania Air National Guard, but their role is one of electronic surveillance and they saw action during the US invasion of Grenada in 1983. Another Hercules on covert operations is the C-130E-II, flown by the 7407th Operational Squadron at Rhein-Main AB in West Germany. Three aircraft are on charge, packed with listening gear and used for eavesdropping flights along the Berlin corridor. Apart from a few small antenna blades these Hercules are extremely inconspicuous. Various other types are also employed occasionally on reconnaissance tasks, such as the Boeing E-3 Sentry and the Boeing EC-135. The latter is normally an airborne command post and radio relay station, yet its electronic communications have apparently been turned to eavesdropping at times.

Maritime reconnaissance is the domain of

the US Navy, and in addition to its regular Lockheed P-3 Orion patrol aircraft the service maintains two squadrons for Sigint duties. VQ-1 based at NAS Agana on Guam and VQ-2 based at Rota in Spain serve the Pacific and Atlantic Fleets respectively, snooping primarily around hostile vessels to map or 'fingerprint' their radar and com-

Lockheed EP-3E Orion

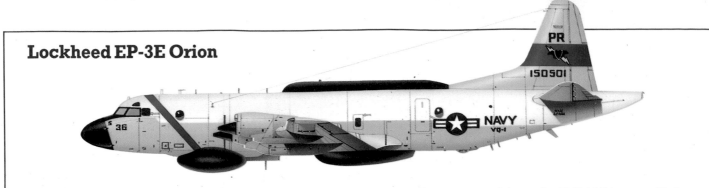

The first electronic reconnaissance versions of the Lockheed Orion were EP-3Bs, which began to replace EC-121s in 1969. The definitive EP-3E version appeared in 1971, and completely replaced the venerable Constellation. The various bulges and blades hide aerials for a comprehensive Sigint suite, making them as capable as the RC-135 in most Sigint disciplines. Their speciality is Elint and Rint, classifying Soviet naval radars for the US Navy. Twelve are in service, split equally between VQ-1 in the Pacific and VQ-2 in the Atlantic and Mediterranean.

Left: The large array of antennae on the EP-3E serves a comprehensive direction-finding, analysis and recording suite in the cabin. Most missions are naval-orientated, with particular accent on Soviet ships and their individual radar fits.

munications suites. Missions are also undertaken against ground targets, the Navy aircraft just as likely to be found flying in the Sea of Okhotsk or off Libya as are their Air Force RC-135 counterparts. The types used by the Navy are still the elderly EA-3B Skywarrior, with its ability to deploy aboard aircraft carriers, and the Lockheed EP-3E Orion. While the Navy looks for a replacement for the Skywarrior, the tired Orions are to be succeeded by further Orions with much lower airframe hours.

On a smaller scale, the US Army is also highly active in electronic surveillance. As recounted earlier, electronic battlefield reconnaissance has become a major part of Army operations, and units are in position in Central America, West Germany and Korea to carry out this role. For the basic Comint and direction finding task, the Army employs the Beech King Air in either its RU-21 or RC-12D versions. The latter is the latest in a long line of Beech special electronic mission aircraft for the Army. Festooned with aerials and dipole antennae, the RC-12D's onboard equipment is fully-automated with a datalink to a ground station. Partnering the RC-12/RU-21 on Army surveillance is the Grumman Mohawk, available in either an OV-1D version for radar and infra-red recon-

Below: In service since 1958, the Douglas EA-3B Skywarrior partners the EP-3E on Sigint missions, deploying on board carriers when necessary. Rapidly approaching the end of their useful lives, the US Navy is searching for a replacement.

Above: Latest in a long line of Beech battlefield Sigint types is the RC-12D 'Guardrail V', which carries fully-automated Comint and Elint equipment in the cabin. Gathered intelligence is transmitted by datalink to ground stations.

Beech RC-12D

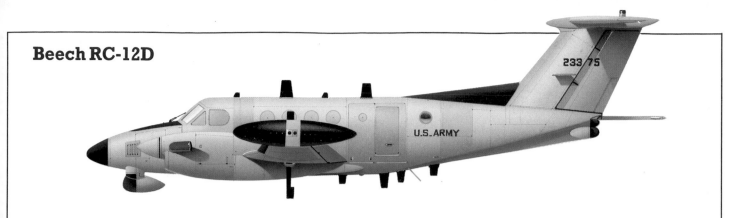

The US Army has employed many small aircraft for the battlefield electronic reconnaissance role, and since the Vietnam war Beech has been the major supplier, with RU-8 and RU-21 serving until the 1980s. The latest is the RC-12D, a version of the civil King Air 200 which drips with aerials and blisters. On board is a fully-automated 'Guardrail V' Comint and direction-finding suite, which relays information to ground stations. RC-12Ds operate alongside Grumman RV-1Ds in Germany and Korea, together providing a complete Comint and Elint surveillance system in both peace and wartime.

naissance, or as an RV-1D Elint platform. The latter features the *Quick Look II* system for classification of hostile radars in the battlefield, both in peacetime and war. Continuing developments keep both RC-12 and RV-1 abreast of Communist advances. A mysterious version of the Beech King Air known as the EU-21A is employed on elec-

Below: Over 100 Grumman OV-1D Mohawks are employed by the US Army on battlefield surveillance, using the pod-mounted radar to peer across the East-West borders. Other specialist sensors include one for measuring radiation levels.

Right: Serving alongside the RC-12D in US Army service is the Grumman RV-1D. This is an Elint specialist carrying the 'Quick Look II' equipment in wingpods and in fuselage modules. Classification of WarPac radars is the primary task.

'Bear-C' and 'Bear-D' (illustrated) versions appeared with a solid tailcone; covering advanced Sigint equipment.

tronic surveillance tasks in Germany, but it is not known what form they take.

Whatever the Soviet Union may lack in technology it more than makes up with num-bers, possessing a huge force of aircraft which are optimized for reconnaissance. Leading the way is the Soviet air force (V-VS) with assets stretching from the giant lumber-ing Tupolev 'Bear' to the Mach 3 'Foxbat'. The latter represents the highest perform-ance available to the Soviet intelligence com-munity, and this enables it to undertake over-flights of nations not equipped with adv-anced SAMs. An estimated 170 MiG-25Rs are in service with the V-VS, but how many are SLAR-equipped 'Foxbat-Ds' is unknown. This version has considerably more strategic applications than the camera-equipped 'Fox-

Tupolev Tu-16 'Badger'

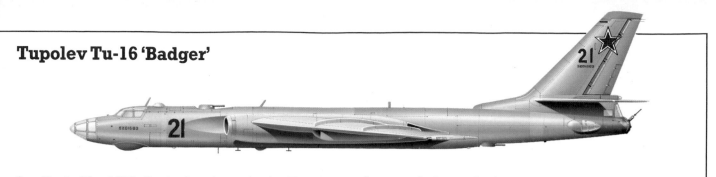

Smallest of the 1950s Soviet bomber trio, the Tupolev Tu-16 first took to the air in 1952, and has provided bombing and missile carrying capability ever since. A large number of variants have been spawned, including several aimed specifically at reconnaissance. The 'Badger-D', 'Badger-F' and 'Badger-K' are configured for Sigint work, and are often caught 'snooping' round NATO ships, classifying their radars and eavesdropping on communications. The 'Badger-E' mounts some Sigint equipment, while also toting several large cameras in the bomb bay for Photint. Nearly 100 Tu-16s are used on reconnaissance duties, flying with all four Soviet Fleets and the air force.

bat-B', being able to fly at great height and speed along a target nation's borders while its radar peers deep inside the enemy territory. In a similar fashion to that of the Lockheed SR-71, Sigint sensors are also carried to provide overall electronic and imagery intelligence. 'Foxbats' have recently been augmented in the strategic reconnaissance role by the MiG-31 'Foxhound'. This new fighter is a derivative of the MiG-25 with far greater manoeuvrability and radar capability, but not able to match the 'Foxbat's' speed or altitude performance. How it performs its strategic reconnaissance role and the nature of its onboard equipment has not yet been released, but large SLARs and Sigint sensors carried in a similar fashion to the MiG-25R seem likely.

Converted bombers

Over a dozen Tupolev Tu-22 'Blinders' also serve the V-VS on strategic reconnaissance duties, this being a supersonic general purpose Sigint and Photint platform, with

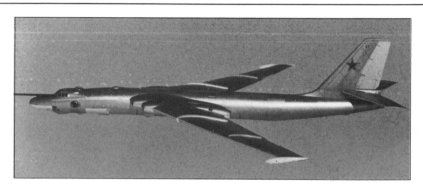

cameras carried in the fuselage bay of this converted bomber. Four Tupolev Tu-95 'Bears' are involved in advanced Sigint work, while the fleet of over 100 Tupolev Tu-16 'Badgers' is split between reconnaissance tasks and active electronic countermeasures. Reconnaissance 'Badgers' are involved in both Sigint and Photint work.

Regularly intercepted by Western fighters, the reconnaissance fleet of the Soviet navy (AV-MF) is almost as large as that of the V-

'Bison-Bs' have made many forays around the Western nations, packed with electronic recording gear to classify naval and air defence radars.

Western interceptors such as these 57th FIS Phantoms have been kept more than busy warding off Soviet spys.

Spyplane

This An-12 is usually used for trials work, but can carry out Sigint work if required. Once again, the aircraft carries spurious Aeroflot markings.

The underfuselage bulge and 'duck-bill' nose radome identify this Tu-16 as a 'Badger-D', a widely-used Sigint platform.

VS. High performance assets rest with the 20 or so Tupolev Tu-22 'Blinder-Cs', often seen over the Baltic and able to photograph and map radar systems of Western vessels in double-quick time. An unknown number of the faster and larger Tupolev Tu-26 'Backfire' can also perform this task, standard bomber aircraft being able to accommodate a camera and electronic sensor pallet in the weapons bay of the aircraft. Workhorse of the naval

reconnaissance fleet however is the Tupolev Tu-16 'Badger', with around 80 aircraft employed on mainly electronic duties. Serving in a number of versions, the 'Badger' is used to monitor Western shipping around the oceans of the world; it is supported by 'Badger-A' tankers, which supply the reconnaissance aircraft with fuel via the unique wingtip-to-wingtip inflight-refuelling method. Giants of the reconnaissance effort are the Tupolev 'Bear' and Myasishchev 'Bison'. Both conceived as long-range bombers, in naval use they are snoopers with the 'Bear' having a secondary missile guidance role. Two versions of the 'Bison' exist, the 'B' and the 'C', and both are regularly intercepted over the Atlantic and North Sea by US and UK fighters. Numbers are dwindling and may be in single figures.

Also decreasing in numbers are the recon-

Ilyushin Il-20 'Coot-A'

A major refit of the Il-18 airliner resulted in the Il-20 'Coot-A', first seen by Western forces in 1978. Many Sigint features are incorporated, together with optical and infra-red sensors. Housed in the giant pod under the fuselage is a SLAR, which presumably can generate imagery of a manner unmatched by other Soviet types. 'Coot-As' do not possess global range, and are consequently encountered over European waters. The British are often intercepting the type in the North Sea and eastern Atlantic as it probes NATO air defence regions. Only a handful of aircraft have so far been converted.

Perhaps the most important Soviet Sigint type is the Ilyushin Il-20 'Coot-A', which is a dedicated conversion of the Il-18 airliner. A small number are in service, with capabilities roughly comparable to the RC-135 or Nimrod R.Mk 1.

Principal equipment of the Il-20 is the ventral SLAR pod and the fuselage side fairing containing infra-red sensors. The large blade aerials are thought to be for satellite communications, while the myriad of other antennae are for Sigint gathering.

naissance-dedicated 'Bears', maybe down to 15 or so. Once the scourge of Western shipping the 'Bears' are still a force to be reckoned with, the 'Bear-C' and 'Bear-D' versions being packed with sensitive electronic gear to re- cord naval radars and communications. Also used on clandestine missions are the 60 Tu-142 'Bear-F' anti-submarine aircraft, and perhaps the 50 Ilyushin Il-38 'May' ASW pat- rollers. US Navy Lockheed Orion ASW air-

Spyplane

A subject of constant updating, the RAF's Nimrod R.Mk 1 fleet now sports a hemp scheme for low visibility both in the air and on the runway. Most of the windows have been blacked out and painted over.

As well as a comprehensive Sigint suite, the Nimrod R.Mk 1 is believed to carry a SLAR mounted in the weapons bay. Missions are usually flown from Wyton, although the type occasionally turns up in Cyprus and Germany.

Recent additions to the Nimrod's equipment fit include hook aerials on the upper fuselage and wing pods. On the wingtips are mounted Loral ESM pods. This is the only aircraft to receive a refuelling probe.

craft have long been suspected of occasionally carrying out other, more secretive, missions, so it seems natural that the sophisticated Soviet aircraft should follow suit, especially as they operate from bases in Libya, South Yemen, Vietnam, Cuba and others.

'Coots' and 'Cubs'

Altogether more important is the Sigint fleet of Ilyushin Il-20 'Coot-As' and Antonov An-12 'Cub-Bs'. Conversions of an airliner and cargo transport respectively, these two types carry vast loads of electronic sensors, operators and language specialists. The 'Cub-B' is believed to be a strict Sigint type, seen in

many different configurations throughout its service career, whereas the 'Coot-A' can generate radar imagery with a large and highly-capable SLAR hung beneath the fuselage. Perhaps around 25 'Cub-Bs' are in service with naval units, supported by a handful of 'Coot-As' which can be likened to the RC-135 in terms of capability. Supporting the Soviet reconnaissance effort are a number of aircraft flying under the flags of Poland, East Germany and Czechoslovakia; these include ancient Ilyushin Il-14 Elint aircraft, Il-28R naval Photint and Elint platforms, and the tactical reconnaissance MiG-21RFs which regularly patrol NATO coasts bordering the Baltic Sea.

Secret Nimrods

The quantitative difference between the Soviet and US reconnaissance fleets is somewhat offset by other Western nations joining in the battle of the airwaves against the Soviet Union. Closest ally to the United States in terms of sharing intelligence and espionage technology is the United Kingdom which, although it only possesses three aircraft dedicated to strategic reconnaissance, produces much intelligence of a highly critical nature. The aircraft in question are the Nimrod R.Mk 1s of No. 51 Sqn, which have been regularly intercepted by Swedish fighters around the Baltic Sea. In common

The Royal Air Force's Canberra PR.Mk 9 strength has been whittled down to five front-line aircraft, serving with 1 Photographic Reconnaissance Unit at Wyton. These aircraft can carry optical and infra-red sensors, and perhaps imaging radar.

with all Western snoopers, they have no doubt been intercepted even more times by Soviet fighters as they go about their shady business. Referred to as 'radar calibration' aircraft by the UK Ministry of Defence, the three Nimrods are extremely secretive, spending their time either on missions or tucked away inside their hangars at Wyton airfield. Operations occasionally take the aircraft to Cyprus and Germany.

Examination of the Nimrod R.Mk 1 reveals an extensive array of antennae that can intercept Soviet communications, while three conical helix antennae are mounted on the tailcone and wings. The large weapons bay of the standard Nimrod has probably been filled with much electronic listening gear in the R.Mk 1 version, perhaps including a SLAR for radar imagery. Also operating from Wyton is the RAF's No. 1 Photographic Reconnaissance Unit, which flies the Canberra PR.Mk 9. As well as providing a useful high-

Canberra PR.Mk 9s have operated from bases in 'hot' areas of the world, notably Hong Kong. At present aircraft are detached to Belize for unspecified purposes.

Swedish interceptors spend as much time escorting western espionage aircraft as their Soviet counterparts. This JA37 Viggen investigates a French Noratlas Elint platform.

Standard maritime patrol aircraft are sometimes used on Sigint missions. France has used Atlantics in this role over war-torn Chad, eavesdropping on the Libyan-backed guerillas.

A single Douglas DC-8 airliner has been modified with electronic reconaissance equipment and flies operational missions over the Baltic to supply France with its own Elint. The wingtip pods may contain a SLAR or Elint detectors.

Above: Italy's Piaggio PD.808 fleet is employed mainly on ECM duties, this one being intercepted by a US Navy F-18 Hornet during a NATO exercise. PD.808s are believed to have a secondary Sigint role.

altitude Photint and infra-red platform, this mark of Canberra has been investigated as a potential carrier for a high-resolution side-looking airborne radar to allow it to operate in a similar fashion to the USAF's TR-1.

Other European nations are equally active in the electronic data gathering role, including France and West Germany. Four of the five special-mission Dassault-Breguet Atlantics delivered to the West German navy's MFG 2 unit are still active over the Baltic on espionage missions. In addition to the characteristic underfuselage fairing, the Sigint Atlantics have sprouted large HF probe ae-

rials under the wings. On board are multi-track recorders and pulse analysers aimed in particular at WarPac radars. Rint equipment may also have been fitted. French strategic reconnaissance missions over the Baltic are mounted by the Escadre Electronique 51 flying from Evreux with a single Douglas DC-8. Occasionally venturing gamely out on similar missions are radial engine-powered Nord Noratlas aircraft, which fly with EE 54 at Metz. Although France is a non-NATO country, it is thought that it is privileged to receive much information gathered by other Western nations.

Italy joins in

The same can also be said of Italy, which has recently joined the ranks of Sigint operators with the introduction of the Aeritalia G.222GE Elint gathering platform. Two aircraft are in service with the 14° Stormo's 71° Gruppo, which also operates a number of Piaggio PD.808GE aircraft on electronic

Dassault-Breguet Atlantic

Another maritime patrol aircraft conversion is the Dassault-Breguet Atlantic, five of which were delivered during the late 1970s to the West German navy for Sigint patrols over the Baltic. Characterised by a large ventral radome, these aircraft carry multi-track recorders and some Rint equipment. Recent additions are large HF probes under the wings. One aircraft has crashed, the remaining four serving with Marinefliegergeschwader 2 at Nordholz alongside standard Atlantics. The French have also used Atlantics in the Sigint role, particularly in Chad.

duties. Final major European strategic reconnaissance nation is non-aligned Sweden, which maintains its two specially-modified Caravelles for electronic surveillance of Soviet activities.

Reconnaissance spreads

Elsewhere in the world the strategic reconnaissance role is catching on fast. Iraq, Libya, Syria and India have all been supplied with reconnaissance versions of the MiG-25 'Foxbat' and these have been used on operational missions against their neighbours. India uses its 'Foxbats' to patrol the borders with Pakistan, while Syria attempts to keep watch on Israel. Iraq flies its aircraft on reconnaissance missions to aid the war with Iran, and Libya has apparently made several 'Foxbat' flights into the territories of Chad and Tunisia.

Out of necessity Israel is a major force in the Middle East region, and to enable it to keep up its highly efficient intelligence war

This innocuous looking aircraft is an Aeritalia G.222 transport suitably modified for the Sigint mission, its main antenna being house in a fin-top radome. Designated G.222GE, this aircraft serves with the 14° Stormo.

against its Arab neighbours it now employs a sizeable fleet of aircraft. Most important of these intelligence gatherers are the unknown number of Boeing 707 Sigint platforms. At least three versions exist, one of which is a dual-purpose Elint gatherer/inflight-refueller. Other aircraft appear to have active jamming capability allied to passive Elint and Comint receivers, while one aircraft has been seen in a configuration bearing a strong re-

Above: In the war with Polisario guerillas, the Moroccan air force employs this SLAR and Sigint equipped Lockheed Hercules. Chief use is patrolling a huge dyke constructed to shield Morocco from guerilla activities.

Spyplane

MiG-25R 'Foxbat-Bs' have been supplied to a small number of nations for reconnaissance purposes, among them Algeria. In service with these nations, the aircraft are often flown and operated by Soviet 'advisers'.

Left: Israel's determination has produced this indigenously-equipped Boeing 707 Sigint platform. An earlier version also features SLARs similar to those carried by USAF RC-135s.

Two Grumman OV-1D Mohawks have been supplied to Israel for surveillance of their Arab neighbours, the pod-mounted SLAR producing imagery across the border. Rumours persist as to the supply of two EV-1E Mohawks, these being dedicated Elint platforms.

semblance to the US Air Force's RC-135V. Of course the C-135 and 707 are very alike, having been derived from the same prototype, and the fitment of similar sensors would pose few engineering problems. Certainly the cheek SLAR fairings and huge underfuselage blade and plate aerials seem to be of the same variety as on the RC-135V, and internal equipment is also likely to be the same, providing the Israelis with one of the most capable Sigint platforms currently flying. Later versions of the Boeing 707 have highlighted Israeli ability to develop and manufacture their own Sigint equipment, instead of relying upon American suppliers. To this end the 707s have acquired an almost complete indigenous avionics fit, including both pas-

sive and active units. Similar equipment has been incorporated in a number of other types in service, including the locally-built IAI Arava utility transport, thus providing a completely Israeli-built aircraft with the capability to perform both Elint and Comint gathering.

Augmenting the Boeing 707s in Israeli service are a number of smaller types of lesser capability, but with no less a part to play in the intelligence effort. Grumman OV-1 Mohawks provide radar and infra-red imagery, and unconfirmed reports suggest that the EV-1 Elint version of the Mohawk has been supplied to Israel. Also unconfirmed, but more likely, is the supply of Beech RU-21s during the mid-1970s and, even if this is not

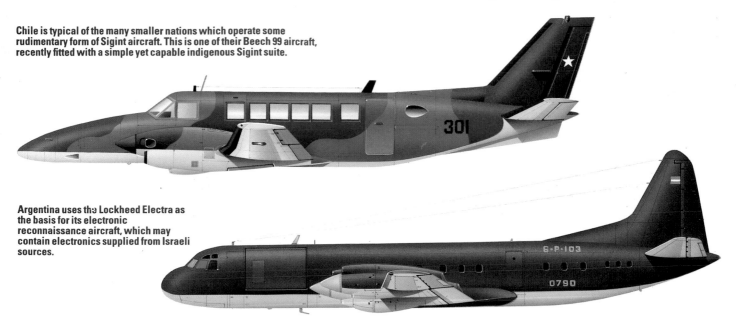

Chile is typical of the many smaller nations which operate some rudimentary form of Sigint aircraft. This is one of their Beech 99 aircraft, recently fitted with a simple yet capable indigenous Sigint suite.

Argentina uses the Lockheed Electra as the basis for its electronic reconnaissance aircraft, which may contain electronics supplied from Israeli sources.

true, standard Queen Airs in Israeli service have more recently been fitted with some Comint gear.

Local products

Some other nations have turned to producing their own avionics to fit into Sigint aircraft, a notable example being Chile which has produced an Elint set to fit into its small Beech 99 aircraft. These provide a measure of reconnaissance capability against Argentina, which in turn operates Lockheed Electras on electronic surveillance missions. Japan also produces its own equipment, albeit with US guidance. Chief Sigint aircraft is the Kawasaki-built version of the Lockheed Neptune, known as the EP-2J when fitted with its reconnaissance gear. Egypt is another notable

nation, having been supplied with a number of EC-130 Hercules for electronic intelligence duties, while little is known of China's intelligence gathering effort, although it can be assumed that a fleet of license-built Tupolev Tu-16s and Ilyushin Il-28s have at least some capability in this direction.

In addition to those mentioned, a whole gamut of nations now operate small utility aircraft equipped with rudimentary listening gear, particularly those with hostile neighbours. Once a game for rich and influential nations, strategic reconnaissance has now become vital to many of lesser importance. It indicates that the role, in particular that of electronic eavesdropping, is now as much a part of today's modern military spectrum as is bombing or air defence.

No details have yet emerged as to a Chinese strategic reconnaissance aircraft, but it seems almost certain such conversions of the Xian H-6 exist. The H-6 is a copy of the Tu-16 'Badger', exemplified here by two standard bombers.

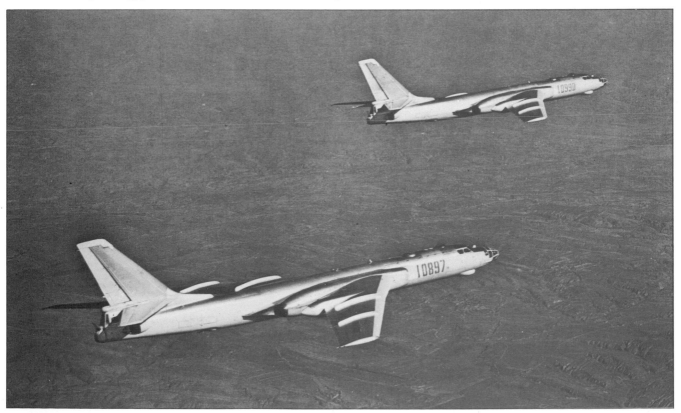

Into the Future

*What does the future have in store for strategic reconnaissance? Certainly there are several strands of development which will greatly affect the role. One now being adopted by the superpower nations is high-altitude stand-off radar reconnaissance, highlighted by Lockheed's **TR-1**. Another more sinister avenue involves the emotive subject of 'stealth'. While details are scarce, the impact this technology could have on strategic reconnaissance cannot be overestimated. Finally, the reconnaissance aircraft will have to interact with ground stations and satellites ever more as these become a major part of surveillance activities.*

Despite the increase in defence capability, the strategic reconnaissance aircraft is still able to operate effectively from stand-off positions as it carries out its vital task, and there seems to be no reduction in the importance of the role. Indeed, as has been seen, there appears to be a steadily growing number of reconnaissance platforms as more and more nations purchase rudimentary Sigint equipment to fit into a variety of aircraft that can spy on their neighbours. So what lies around the corner for strategic reconnaissance?

Obviously the trend towards lightweight Sigint aircraft is set to continue as further nations deem the acquisition of a listening post necessary to their defences. Of course,

such aircraft have been used by the superpowers since the early 1950s, and these nations are set to take the reconnaissance aircraft into new eras. One avenue now in service, and set to become a major facet in the operations of a large air force is that of continuous high-altitude surveillance, as now practised by the Lockheed TR-1. The recent advent of high-resolution synthetic aperture radars allows the TR-1 to patrol the West German border for hours on end, the onboard sensors automatically peering into East German territory to spot any military movements or advances. Data gleaned in such a method is datalinked back to ground stations for near real-time analysis, allowing NATO commanders to have an up-to-the-minute picture of

Spyplane

The TR-1 is a high-value target during wartime due to its immense value to ground commanders. Consequently, it is fitted with a comprehensive radar warning and ECM suite to protect it from hostile SAMs

WarPac military intentions and readiness. These as yet unique capabilities provide intelligence that can be extremely useful at local level during wartime, and as such can be labelled tactical, but this data can be as useful at national or strategic level. In addition, Comint and Elint sensors can be carried by the TR-1 (either by themselves for coverage across a wide frequency band, or in addition to the airborne radars) to provide a complete picture of the situation, the latter being most desirable for the staff plotting enemy intentions.

High-performance sensors

Blessed with excellent endurance and altitude performance inherited from its U-2R forebear, the TR-1 is still only as effective as its sensors, and these must keep pace with advances made in the targets they seek. Airborne radars are now producing higher-re-

solution imagery than ever before, while the TR-1, SR-71 and U-2R still retain the capability to carry huge folding-optics cameras which can provide unbelievable photographs at oblique distances of up to 75 miles (120 km). Sigint equipment is under continual refinement, and equally important is the constant improvement to the huge ground-based computers (found at such places as the CIA and National Security Agency) which decode the raw encrypted data gathered by strategic reconnaissance aircraft.

While the TR-1 is the first of a new breed, others are set to follow and already the US Air Force is working on a similar programme to augment the TR-1s. This is the Boeing E-8, a converted 707 airliner carrying the giant J-STARS radar which performs a similar task to that equipping the TR-1s, but from lower level. The high level mission has been in-

This Lockheed U-2R was used for tests of TR-1 equipment. Principal among these is the ASARS radar system, which is now operational on the TR-1A. This accounts for the bizarre extended nose.

vestigated by the United Kingdom, using the CASTOR radar on board a Canberra PR.Mk 9 to perform a similar function to the TR-1. In the Soviet Union a prototype of a high-altitude reconnaissance platform has been noted. Bearing a close resemblance to the TR-1, the 'Ram-M' (as it is known to NATO) is no doubt to be used for the same stand-off high-altitude continuous surveillance task.

Invisible aircraft

An altogether more sinister avenue for the strategic reconnaissance aircraft to follow has been the subject of many secret projects undertaken since the 1950s. Low observability, or the so-called 'stealth' technique, involves rendering an aircraft less visible to the spectrum of detection equipment available to the defences. The chief sensor in current use is radar, and the designers of 'stealth' aircraft are primarily concerned with reducing the radar cross-section that they present. This is achieved in a number of ways, the most radical of which is by shaping the aircraft in such a way as to vastly reduce the radio pulse reflected back to the defence radar. Blended surfaces, elimination of flat plane surfaces and careful shrouding of engine inlets all reduce reflected radar beams, while the internal structure is built on anechoic principles, using triangles and honeycomb structures, to 'capture' radar energy within them, bouncing it around until it is dissipated rather than reflected back to the receiver.

Special materials

Low radar cross-sections are also achieved by the use of special non-metallic materials, which absorb or distort radar energy, and they are of particular importance when used on the aircraft skin and around the large metallic mass of the engines. Such techniques have been secretly tested for years, more and more radar-absorbing material (RAM)

British interest in an airborne surveillance radar rests on the CASTOR unit to be carried perhaps by the Canberra PR.Mk 9. This aircraft features a bulge under the fuselage, which may contain a CASTOR-type radar.

The Hughes ASARS radar enables the U-2R/TR-1 to monitor enemy armoured formations far behind their front line, so warning NATO ground commanders of reinforcements long before they arrive at the front.

Lockheed TR-1A

First flying on 1 August 1981, the TR-1A is essentially a modernised U-2R, utilising the same structure with updated systems. 14 of the new aircraft have gone to England to form the 17th Reconnaissance Wing at Alconbury, with a primary tasking of high-altitude radar surveillance of WarPac territory, for which they carry the ASARS radar. Others serve with the 9th SRW at Beale in California on several tasks, alongside the remaining U-2Rs. Included in the production run were two TR-1B trainers, with a second cockpit in the Q-bay area.

Keith Fretwell.

Spyplane

Apart from the tremendous heat generated by the engines and the large slab fins, the Lockheed SR-71 is an excellent 'stealth' design, with blended chines and engine nacelles. Incorporated into the leading and trailing edges of the wing are wedges of radar absorbent material, arranged in triangles to bounce radar energy within them to fully absorb it. Alternating with the RAM is the titanium structure of the wing.

This is how one artist sees the Lockheed 'Stealth' fighter, wearing black paint to render it less visible. Of more importance is the overall design of the aircraft to reduce noise, infra-red and radar signatures.

being used as scientists develop lighter and more efficient substances. Lockheed U-2s were tested with RAM early in their career, as have been certain 'British reconnaissance aircraft' (probably Canberras). Stealth techniques surfaced during the drone operations in South East Asia, some aircraft being configured with a mesh structure across the engine inlet to shield the highly-reflective compressor blades of the engine, and also carrying other RAM elements. Of course the Lockheed SR-71 incorporates much early stealth technology, its shape alone (apart from the giant slab fins) proving a difficult target for radar beams. In the leading edge of the wing can be spotted anechoic triangles of RAM, framed by the titanium structure of the aircraft. Electronic interference with the radar waves by onboard equipment, known as deception electronic countermeasures, is also used to give confusing or spurious radar returns.

Radar is not the only method of aircraft detection, and stealth aircraft must have shrouded engines with high-bypass turbofans to reduce noise to a minimum. Equally important is heat emission, which also has to be drastically reduced to prevent detection by infra-red sensors. Heat absorbing material is packed around the engine and cool air mixed with the exhaust to spread the large emission of heat over a greater area. Finally the aircraft must not give away its position by emissions of its own. Radar cannot be carried as this could be detected by passive receivers, so passive equipment must be used for navigation and terrain avoidance. Forward-looking infra-red has a large part to play in this, and perhaps new avionics such as laser radars. Global navigation would be handled by satellite and star-tracking systems, allied to inertial navigation.

Early research

Current stealth programmes can be traced back to the early 1970s, and originated in the Lockheed 'Skunk Works' from which had issued the U-2 and SR-71. Low observability features had been incorporated into the A-12, SR-71 and D-21 drone programmes, so the secret Lockheed department had gained much experience in these techniques. In 1973 the US Air Force received an innocuous looking lightplane from an American aircraft designer who had been working on low-RCS and glassfibre aircraft. Known as the Windecker YE-5A, this lightplane was extensively tested by various agencies, including the 'Skunk Works', to evaluate its stealth techniques. Covered by a dielectric skin, the YE-5A featured considerable amounts of internal RAM, particularly around the engine and cockpit.

Ultra-secret prototype

Experience from this and previous projects gave Lockheed enough data to build a small-scale stealth fighter under the codename *Have Blue*, which began flight tests from Groom Lake in early 1977. A number were built and extensively tested within the vast

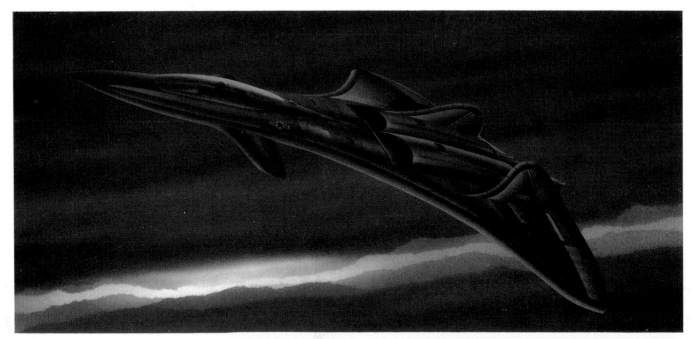

The low profile of the 'Stealth' fighter has little radar cross-section from the side, and even less from the front. The small fins help to shroud the inevitable heat emissions from the engines.

Nellis ranges in Nevada. These XST vehicles gave way to a full size stealth aircraft in 1982, which joined those being evaluated at Groom Lake. Since that time a fleet of such aircraft has been operating from the nearby Tonopah base, reportedly deploying around the world in C-5 Galaxy transports. The official acronym applied to these aircraft is COSIRS, or covert survivable in-weather reconnaissance/strike. How much of the 'strike' is currently used is unknown, but these aircraft have been deployed on reconnaissance missions although no details have been forthcoming. The traditional US Air Force operating locations for clandestine missions, namely Alaska, Japan and England, appear to have been visited by these aircraft, subject of the most secret project in the history of aviation. The advantages of low-observability aircraft to the strategic reconnaissance role are plain to see. If the aircraft cannot be detected until close to ground sites, it can penetrate much farther into hostile airspace, while on peripheral missions an enemy's ground bases will not be alerted to the spy's presence, so allowing it to gain information about air defence systems perhaps not available to the conventional snooper. As with many other US projects, the Soviet Union has realised the benefits of such a system and is developing its own stealth aircraft, perhaps to fulfil a similar reconnaissance role.

Aircraft are by no means the only way of collecting the intelligence required by

A little known aircraft involved in 'stealth' research was the Windecker YE-5A. Built from dielectric fibre glass materials, the YE-5A was tested with radar absorbent material internally, packed particularly around the large metal mass of the engine.

Another 'stealth' design shows the shrouded and dorsally mounted engines. Aircraft such as this have great capabilities in the reconnaissance role, being able to penetrate defences to a far greater degree than conventional designs.

national agencies. Traditional Humint methods are as important as ever, while ground-based stations are also eavesdropping on hostile communications traffic. Installations such as the UK's GCHQ and numerous US listening posts around the world monitor Communist and Arab radio traffic, while other ground installations such as giant radars also help the overall intelligence effort. Airborne spies regularly combine with these ground-based sensors, and their respective operations are mutually supporting rather than being in competition. A classic example is the *Cobra Dane* radar based on Shemya island, from where also fly the RC-135S aircraft of the 6th SW. Both are employed in concert on surveillance of the Soviet ICBM programme, occasionally assisted by shipborne sensor systems, such as the *Cobra Judy* radar or Sigint listening posts sailing off hostile shores.

Perhaps the biggest threat to the strategic reconnaissance aircraft has come from the spy satellite, which can provide both excellent Photint or Sigint from orbits in space.

Reconnaissance Platform Operating Heights

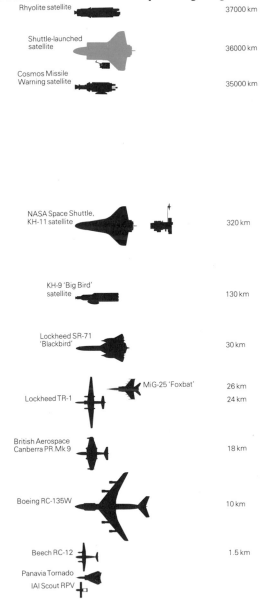

Rhyolite satellite	37000 km
Shuttle-launched satellite	36000 km
Cosmos Missile Warning satellite	35000 km
NASA Space Shuttle, KH-11 satellite	320 km
KH-9 'Big Bird' satellite	130 km
Lockheed SR-71 'Blackbird'	30 km
MiG-25 'Foxbat'	26 km
Lockheed TR-1	24 km
British Aerospace Canberra PR.Mk 9	18 km
Boeing RC-135W	10 km
Beech RC-12	1.5 km
Panavia Tornado	
IAI Scout RPV	

The use of satellites allows direct overflights of target nations for Photint missions, while other satellites sit in geosynchronous orbits to listen in on all forms of communications. Despite the threat to the operations of reconnaissance aircraft, the two have operated side-by-side since the early 1960s, and the merits of both systems seem too great for either to be discarded. 1961 saw the first US reconnaissance satellite in orbit, followed a year later by a Soviet craft. Both nations now employ a number of types, which at regular intervals eject data capsules over friendly territory. Recent developments have allowed the satellites to relay their intelligence to ground stations by means of digital datalink. While Soviet satellites are grouped under the all-embracing 'Cosmos' label, rendering individual identification difficult, the United States is known to operate the following types. The KH-9 'Big Bird' is a photo satellite which may also carry a radar to produce imagery. The KH-11 is another photo-recon craft with datalink capability, while the KH-8 is an older design, with no datalink. For Sigint duties the 'White Cloud' and 'Rhyolite' systems are used, the latter flying at some 22,500 miles (36200 km) from the earth. Other smaller Sigint satellites are also employed to keep watch on northern Soviet bases and a specialist Telint satellite is in use. In addition to the Soviet Union and United States, China has been operating spy satellites since 1975, and the United Kingdom looks set to introduce an independent European Sigint satellite capability with its project 'Zircon'.

Moving forward together

For a quarter of a century the spy satellite and strategic reconnaissance aircraft have existed together, strengthening each other's particular talents. Whatever the advances made to satellite and ground-based intelligence gathering sensors, the aircraft will always be one of the prime vehicles for strategic reconnaissance, able to provide a rapid response in any area of the world and with a wide array of sensors to cover any eventuality. For many years to come the deadly game of aerial espionage will continue, especially around the borders of NATO, the Soviet Union, in Central America and the Middle East. The Cold War is far from over.

Above: This enormous phased array radar installation is located on the US outpost of Shemya, at the end of the Aleutian chain. Its role is surveillance of Soviet missile tests, which it shares with the 6th SW's RC-135S and RC-135X fleet which operates from the same base.

Far left: The diagram shows the reconnaissance spectrum in terms of altitude, ranging from low level drones operating at tree-top height to the remote Sigint satellites at thousands of miles distant. Although performing many of the same tasks as air-breathing aircraft, satellites and reconnaissance aircraft complement each other, and no dual user has lessened its reliance on aircraft since the introduction of spacecraft.

Right: Despite the severe setback to military programmes caused by the tragic loss of the Space Shuttle 'Challenger', the United States is preparing for a large reconnaissance satellite launching programme from Shuttles. The vehicle itself can also provide useful intelligence from orbit, while repairing and replenishing older satellites. Shown is 'Challenger', before its fateful mission.

INDEX

Page numbers in **bold** indicate an illustration

An asterisk (*) signifies a reference to a colour profile

Unless indicated otherwise, all entries in italics are codenames of missions, programmes or systems

Index

Myasishchev
Mya-4 'Bison': 38, **40***, 71, 72, 74, 106
Mya-4 'Bison-B': 40, **74**, **105**, 106
Mya-4 'Bison-C' 40, 72, **74**, 106

N

NASA (National Aeronautics & Space Administration): 42, 43
NATO (North Atlantic Treaty Organisation) 38, 71, 75, 105, 107, 108, 110, 115, 117, 122
N.C.701 Martinet (see Nord)
Neptune, AP-2E (see Lockheed)
Neptune, P2V (see Lockheed)
Neptune, RB-69A (see Lockheed)
Neptune, RP-2E (see Lockheed)
Nimitz, USS: 81
Nimrod (see British Aerospace)
Nixon, President Richard M: 34
Noratlas (see Nord)
Nord
N.C.701 Martinet: 53, **53**
Noratlas: 88, **89**, **109**, 110
North American RB-45C Tornado: **17**, 18, 19, **19**

O

'Open Skies' policy: 27
Operation 'Litterbug': 68
Orion, EP-3B (see Lockheed)
Orion, P-3 (see Lockheed)
Otter, RU-1 (see de Havilland Canada)
OV-1 Mohawk (see Grumman)
OV-1D (see Grumman)

P

P2V Neptune (see Lockheed)
P-3 Orion (see Lockheed)
P4M Mercator (see Martin)
P-38 Lightning (see Lockheed)
Pave Nickel: 78, 79
Pave Onyx: 78, 79
PB4Y Privateer (see Consolidated)
PD.808 (see Piaggio)
PD.808GE (see Piaggio)
Peenemünde: 11
Phantom (see McDonnell Douglas)

Phantom, RF-4 (see McDonnell Douglas)
Phoenix, AIM-54A (see Hughes)
Photint (photographic intelligence): 8, 15, 16, 17, 18, 19, 24, 27, 31, 36, 41, 60, 63, 67, 75, 86, 88, 91, 95, 105, 108, 110, 122
Piaggio
PD.808: **110**
PD.808GE: 110
Poland
Air Force: 89
Polisario guerrillas: 111
Powers, Francis Gary: 15, 27, 29, 31, 32, 34, 35
Pratt & Whitney
J57: 26, 27, 29, 47, 54
J58: 42
J60: 40
J75: 29, 42
TF33: 40, 55
Privateer, PB4Y (see Consolidated)
Pueblo, USS: 49

Q

QRC-259 superhetrodyne receiver: 47
Queen Air (see Beech)
Quick Look II: 103

R

RAM (radar absorbing material): 117, 120
'Ram-M' reconnaissance aircraft: 117
Ravens: 24, 36, 46, 48, 54
RB-29 (see Boeing)
RB-29A (see Boeing)
RB-36 (see Convair)
RB-36F (see Convair)
RB-45C Tornado (see North American)
RB-47 (see Boeing)
RB-47E (see Boeing)
RB-47H (see Boeing)
RB-50 (see Boeing)
RB-57A (see Martin)
RB-57D (see Martin)
RB-57F (see Martin)
RB-66 (see Douglas)
RB-66C (see Douglas)
RB-69 (see Lockheed)

RB-69A (see Lockheed)
RC-12 (see Beech)
RC-12D (see Beech)
RC-130A (see Lockheed)
RC-135 (see Boeing)
RC-135C (see Boeing)
RC-135D (see Boeing)
RC-135E (see Boeing)
RC-135M (see Boeing)
RC-135S (see Boeing)
RC-135U (see Boeing)
RC-135V (see Boeing)
RC-135W (see Boeing)
RC-135X (see Boeing)
Reconnaissance Systems Officer (RSO) 45, 46
Republic
F-84F: 25
RF-84K: 24, 26
RF-4 Phantom (see McDonnell Douglas)
RF-84K (see Republic)
RF-101C Voodoo (see McDonnell)
RF-104 Starfighter (see Lockheed)
'Rhyolite' Sigint system: 122
Rint (radiation intelligence) 9, 80, 95, 96, 102, 110, 111
RP-2E Neptune (see Lockheed)
RPV (remotely piloted vehicle) 64, 68
RU-1 Otter (see de Havilland Canada)
RU-6 Beaver (see de Havilland Canada)
RU-8 Seminole (see Beech)
RU-21 (see Beech)
RV-1 (see Grumman)
RV-1D (see Grumman)
Ryan
AQM-34 (147): 65
AQM-34L: 67, **67**, 68
AQM-34M(L): **67**
AQM-34Q: 65, 67
AQM-34R: 65, **66**, 67
Firebee 1: 64

S

S-1010B pressure suit: 98
SA-2 'Guideline': 28, 31, 32, 34, 40, 61, **63**, 65, 66, 67, 78
Saab
JA37 Viggen: **109**
Viggen: 86
'Scan Odd' radar: 21
Schalk, Lou: 42
Schwalbe (see Messerschmitt Me 262)

Seaberg, Major John; 26, 27
Seminole, RU-8 (see Beech)
Senior Book: 63
Sentry, E-3 (see Boeing)
Sigint (signals intelligence) 8, 12, 15, 16, 17, 18, 19, 20, 21, 22, 23, 24, 26, 27, 28, 31, 34, 36, 37, 40, 46, 47, 48, 51, 53, 54, 56, 58, 59, 60, 61, 62, 63, 65, 71, 72, 75, 76, 77, 78, 79, 80, 81, 82, 85, 86, 88, 89, 90, 95, 96, 100, 101, 102, 105, 106, 107, 108, 110, 111, 112, 113, 115, 116, 122
Sikorsky
CH-3: 65
CH-3E: **66**
'Skunk Works': 41, 120
Skyknight, EF-10B (see Douglas)
Skywarrior, EA-3 (see Douglas)
SLAR (side-looking airborne radar) 22, 47, 51, 55, 56, 61, 75, 77, 78, 82, 88, 96, 104, 105, 107, 108, 109, 110, 111, 112
Soviet Union
Air Force: 104, 105, 106
KGB: 32
Naval Aviation: 105
Space Shuttle: 122
Spitfire (see Supermarine)
SR-71 (see Lockheed)
SR-71A (see Lockheed)
SR-71B (see Lockheed)
Starfighter, F-104 (see Lockheed)
Starfighter, RF-104 (see Lockheed)
Starlite night vision scope: 89
'Stealth' fighter (see Lockheed)
Stealth techniques: 117, 120, 121
Stratocruiser, EC-97G (see Boeing)
Stratofortress, B-52H (see Boeing)
Stratojet, B-47 (see Boeing))
Stratolifter, C-135 (see Boeing)
Stratotanker, KC-135 (see Boeing)
Su -21 'Flagon' (see Sukhoi)
Suez crisis: 27, 28
Sukhoi Su-21 'Flagon': 93, **93**
Superfortress, B-29 (see Boeing)
Supermarine
Spitfire: 9, 10, 12
Spitfire Mk I: **8**
Spitfire Mk V: 10
Spitfire PR.Mk X: **10**
Spitfire PR.Mk XI: **8**, **11**
Sweden
Air Force: 84
F13 Wing: 88
Forsokcentralen: 86, 88